T0021370

DROP
THE **BS**
(BELIEF SYSTEMS)
AND **BE**

KELI ADAMS

authorHOUSE®

AuthorHouse™
1663 Liberty Drive
Bloomington, IN 47403
www.authorhouse.com
Phone: 1 (800) 839-8640

Published by AuthorHouse 09/24/2019

ISBN: 978-1-7283-2858-4 (sc)
ISBN: 978-1-7283-2856-0 (hc)
ISBN: 978-1-7283-2857-7 (e)

Library of Congress Control Number: 2019915054

Print information available on the last page.

*Any people depicted in stock imagery provided by Getty Images are models,
and such images are being used for illustrative purposes only.
Certain stock imagery © Getty Images.*

*"From Ultimate Journey" and "Robert Monroe's Affirmation"
used by permission from The Monroe Institute
365 Roberts Mountain Road
Faber, Virginia 22938
434-361-1500 Office
434-361-1237 Fax*

This book is printed on acid-free paper.

I have created false names for all of the characters, (deceased or alive), businesses (all are nonexistent now), as well as the location of the small Pennsylvania town where I lived (everyone in this story moved or died long ago), that may be recognized.

I am using my real name. After all, it IS my story, all true, with experiences and events that really happened. My mother, Marilyn, is very real and has given me permission to use her name in this book.

All news events are compilations of printed media and television news reports, and have been paraphrased to simply give the reader information about these events.

The Monroe Institute, mentioned in this book, has given me full written permission to use any of their copyrighted information in order to promote their amazing work.

INTRODUCTION

In this book, I am going to tell you many things. I will tell you a bit about me, my beginnings, and many amazing, indescribable and life-changing experiences I have had in my life, and continue to have every day. I want you to get acquainted with me, my personality, and some of my life history that makes me who I am today. Then you may resonate with what I am going to introduce you to later on in the book that will enable you to have your own amazing, indescribable and life-changing experiences...if you choose to.

We assign importance or value to people, events, things, and experiences based on our opinions, judgments, and perceptions. Reality begins and ends with the observer. I will show you how to "observe" differently in order to change your reality and manifest change on many levels. What's really cool about this is that you will be able to feel physical sensations, experiencing emotional and mental shifts and changes. Be open to receive. It's that simple.

How do you "observe" differently? By not looking. Open and allow Source to provide whatever it knows you need the most, be it physical, emotional, mental healing for yourself or others. You will receive as much as your perception allows.

Our perceptions create our beliefs and ideas, which creates our reality. It's a very good thing that perceptions are negotiable, and that reality can change as quickly as a simple shift in our "observing" differently, opening and letting go in order to receive.

I will introduce you to **"din-A-be,"** the simple yet powerful key that shows you how to easily shift perceptions in order to connect with **SOELI** (Source of Energy-Light-Information) for deep healing and instantaneous transformation. You see how to **DROP** in order to tap into the infinite potential to help yourself as well as others.

The last part of the book is the most interesting, at least for me. This section is comprised of transmissions directly from "God," the "Creator," "Divine Intelligence," "SOELI."

How dare I claim that I am receiving information directly from "God," you ask? Why not? Anyone who prays is talking to God. The trick is in knowing when to be still and listen. In the craziness of the world today, it doesn't seem as if many people are hearing much of what spirit is telling them, but paying more attention to what the ego wants. You see where it gets us.

So, by getting out of the way, having no knowledge of what is being said, I simply become God's secretary, typing whatever flows from Source into my computer. Automatic writing and my mindless typing conveys the information that **"SOELI,"** the **S**ource **O**f **E**nergy, **L**ight and **I**nformation deems pertinent for us at this time. Since I am merely the typist for God, I have no idea what is being said. Until this book is published and I read it for the first time just like you, I am clueless as to what **SOELI** has offered. How fun is that?

We all may learn something.

HI THERE

This book has swirled and morphed over the past few months, creating its own unique personality with interesting qualities all its own. What I had in mind for it is nothing like what it has turned into. Like so many tiny fireflies blinking off and on in the silent darkness of a warm summer night, ideas of what I wanted to write zipped around in my mind at all hours of the day and night.

I love to write. I am not concerned about whether people think I am a "good" writer or whether I am going to make a lot of money from my books. To me, a "good" book is simply a book that I enjoy reading...that entertains me...allows me to learn something new...one that I can wiggle down into the space between the lines on the pages...a book that I don't want to end.

Besides, my books simply start churning their way to the surface of my mind like a little kid poking you in the middle of an important conversation. They won't leave me alone until I write them and have completed them to THEIR satisfaction. It's best for me not to ignore the creative "nudges" I get if I want to get any sleep at all.

So here I offer another one of my creations and the most fun of my books to date. I love all of them.

This book is a swirling, liquid kaleidoscope of experiences and events in my life that make me who and what I am today. Is it all true? You bet.

In this book, I am going to tell you stories that I have never told anyone my entire life. There are things that I became aware of as a child that I have held safely in the recesses of my memory, holding it all in check. Until now.

With the intuitive gifts I have opened up to over the years, perceptions I have adopted as true to me, and embracing my "quirkiness," those childhood experiences have opened like a magnificent rose, the fragrance of my fringe life wafting out, ready to be experienced by others.

Ever since I was a young girl, (and most likely as a result of my young childhood experiences and the need to understand "things" that happened to me), I have always been curious about all things metaphysical, paranormal, unusual, fringe, holistic, and outside the "norm." ET's, UFO's, sasquatch, ancient aliens and civilizations, eastern philosophies, bizarre and unusual places, and alternative healing modalities, all became my obsessions and fields of study. And still I felt a restlessness of something I needed to "find," to discover, an itch I couldn't scratch.

For a period of about 5 years in 1988, I began my sojourn into becoming trained, certified and "mastered" in many alternative healing modalities, techniques, and methods...to the point that I had so many certificates I could have papered a wall. I became a Reiki master/teacher. I have taken training in the Silva Method, NLP, hypnosis, Therapeutic Touch, Matrix Energetics, the Reconnection, Remote Viewing, out-of-body travel and astral projection. I became a grief counselor using Raymond Moody's Psychomanteum method of mirror-gazing therapy, a hospice volunteer, a trainer for NODA (No One Dies Alone), and an end of life death doula (coach). What I didn't train in, I read about voraciously, drinking in all I could about so many things and devouring the information I received. And still I felt a restlessness of something I needed to "find," to discover, an itch I couldn't scratch. I am not going to water down the story with information about all of these modalities. You can research them for yourself. I gained a great deal from all of them, grateful for all that I received in order to help others and learn about myself. Each modality has brought me closer to myself and where I am today.

People know that I have developed some unique "gifts" over the years, allowing me the ability to help people in wonderful and amazing ways. I will not go into all of those now as I want to stay on point for the book. You can find me on the internet if you are interested in researching me for yourself.

I want to focus now on all of those events and experiences from my young life that have connected the dots to the woman and the spirit that I have become. No one knows of the things that I have kept to myself for decades until I was able to comprehend them myself as I began remembering things, unveiling possible reasons behind things that I experienced (and am still experiencing in my adult life), and having some kind of "knowingness" as to what it all means. Little threads of past memories and added new experiences on an almost daily basis are opening amazing portals of perception to me that I will never be able to explain or describe. I'm not even going to begin to attempt to do so. I'm just going to enjoy the ride.

Most people know the basics of me; my family and a couple of close friends know a bit more than other folks. In this book, I will share some more of the many layers of events and experiences I have disclosed to no one that make me who I am, creating the "glue" of my life.

Why now, after decades of not "sharing" with a single soul? For one thing, I wasn't aware of much of it until the past handful of years and didn't know what to do with it myself. Terrifying at times when I was a child, beyond my comprehension most of the time growing up, and fascinating always as an adult, I now jump on the magic carpet with playful enthusiasm and ask, "Where to next?!"

Up until the past few years, the gifts that I have, the things that I can do, haven't (and for some folks, still aren't) been readily accepted by a great deal of people in this country.

Working as a flight attendant for a large American airline since 1986, and not wanting to be called in for a psych evaluation if I scared the dickens out of a co-worker with some fantastic story from my life, I have kept most of my life to myself. I am still a flight attendant for a large American airline (it keeps me grounded) and will retire when I no longer want to do it any longer.

Why do I all of the sudden want to disclose some of the interesting and weird "glue" of my life now? Several reasons. I am beyond the point of caring what people think of me and what I do. Not attached to their thoughts, opinions, judgments or beliefs. I'm blissfully happy being me, offering what I have to offer with my quirky fringe gifts, and no one getting hurt along the way.

Another good reason has to do with where our society is today. My life has nothing on some of the "reality" shows on TV these days that people are obsessed with. My quirky fringe blends right in.

The biggest reason for coming out with some of my bizarre life experiences has to do with timing. And the time is now for people like me to come forward as messengers and way showers, remembering experiences from out past that are coming to the surface as information to pass on to others in a time when the world needs it the most.

Quantum physics is bringing God, science and consciousness MUCH closer together, and is truly amazing and exciting stuff. It helps me understand my gifts. It also helps me comprehend "how" we are how we are, how our thoughts create our realities. I'm not even going to attempt to contemplate the "why." That will make anyone crazy.

Several years ago, while searching for something that would "explain" me to me, quantum physics got my attention and "I" began to make sense to "ME." With the curiosity of a hungry child I started reading, studying, eating everything I could about quantum physics, entanglement, photons, string theory, everything I had no clue about and do NOT understand. I am not a physicist, scientist or a mathematician. I barely made it through pre-math in college and almost blew up my lab partner in chemistry class. Quantum physics is pretty heady stuff and goes deeper into realms of "holy crap" than my imagination can grasp. However, I DO know how to "play" with quantum physics without the need to understand. And I show people how to play in order to manifest pretty amazing things in their lives.

God, science, and consciousness entangled and playing nicely with each other. And easily accessible to EVERYONE by simply getting out of your head, trusting, allowing, and letting go.

Once I gave up the need to "understand" or to know "why" things are the way they are, to have an explanation for everything, the fun really started and amazing things began happening in my life. New abilities began presenting themselves to me, allowing me to help others on even deeper levels. I was now able to describe to people all of my intuitive psychic "stuff" in simple scientific terms that make sense. By simply BEING and not really DOING anything, quantum mechanics enhances all that I already am...becoming more intuitive, insightful, and a more efficient healing facilitator on very deep levels. Magic happens. Miraculous transformation happens. The true magic is that EVERYONE can do this if they just get out of their heads and play.

To not be concerned about what others think or believe, to not have to feel "normal" or fit in, to be able to offer simple yet amazing things to people that seem to manifest instantaneous and powerful transformation for healing...now that is fun!!! And it is absolutely freeing for the soul to live your own truth and no one else's illusion. What others THINK you NEED to be or NEED to do is none of your business. Live your own truth without attachment to anything...with a childlike sense of trust, wonder, curiosity, grace, gratitude and love. Do this and you will know that God (whatever/whoever that may be to you) has got your back. BE instead of DO. Allow yourself to get "unstuck" and out of your head and your perception will shift to one of divine mind...and into a space of play, joy, grace, healing, miracles and unlimited possibility.

I would be remiss if I didn't also mention the magic of The Monroe Institute, located in beautiful Faber, VA (about 40 minutes south of Charlottesville.) I read all of Robert Monroe's books about out-of-body travel and life beyond death in the early 1990's. I attended my first Gateway Voyage in 1999 and was hooked. I have attended about 30 of the powerful 6-day residential programs to date. For me, attending a TMI program is like going to Disneyworld after dark, having the entire park to yourself to safely explore other states of consciousness, to explore outside the limitations of physical 3D humanness. When we get expansive and go "outside" ourselves, we discover the magic and wonder of who we truly are "inside." It is here where all healing is available for ourselves as well as for others. I've done a lot of personal healing on many levels as a result of the TMI programs I have taken. This in turn has expanded my gifts to serve others much more profoundly.

I have included more information about The Monroe Institute at the end of the book with express permission by them to use this information. Check it out for yourselves. Read Bob Monroe's books. Take advantage of the powerful programs and healing offerings they have.

For now...
I hope you enjoy the book.

AND NOW...

All About Me

(Gotta Start Somewhere)

Extroverts are people who feel lonely **without** a crowd.
Introverts feel lonely **in** one.
I hate crowds.
I am quite "sociable," just no so "social."
Enough said.

Take all the intuitive gifts I have embraced over the decades, all
of the experiences I am going to share with you, throw in the fierce
introverted soul that I am, and you have quite a tangle of "interesting."

Have fun!

CHAPTER 1

1963

Jolted out of a dreamless sleep in the middle of the night, the sense of suspended animation overpowers me once again. Hearing the panicky beating of my heart pounding like a frightened animal, all I can do is lie here and wait for what I know is coming. I'm keeping my eyes closed tightly as I always do; not wanting to see whatever "it" was that had been interrupting my dream-time for the past several months.

I feel the deadly silence before it even gets here. Deeper than deep sleep itself, the unsettling shift in the quiet of the night is wrapping itself around me as it has been doing for so many nights, paralyzing me in a state of frozen terror of what was still in store for me. I want so desperately to scream, to run, to hide, to become invisible. I can't move a muscle or make a sound. The terrifying vacuum-like stillness has me pinned down with nothing but my raw terror to let me know that I am alive and that this is really happening.

The locust-like buzzing begins at the far end of the hallway. Faint at first, it gets louder as it comes down the hall toward my room, turning into a strange hum by the time it drifts through the doorway, floating up into the far corner toward the ceiling, just hovering there. I am too terrified to open my eyes and look. If I keep my eyes closed maybe it won't "see" me. Since I am numb and not able to move anyhow, maybe it will think I'm dead and leave me alone.

In an instant I find myself sitting straight up in bed, drenched in sweat, disoriented but very focused, eyes open and gazing at a spot of light the size of a golf ball on the middle of the small wall between my bedroom door and my closet. I am involuntarily transfixed by this light that seems to be undulating and shimmering with otherworldly luminosity, and slowly growing to a size roughly 3 feet tall and 2 feet wide. Looking like brilliant moonlight reflecting off the surface of a dark rippling pond, it seems to pulsate brighter and brighter as it grows. I can't help being mesmerized by this light, drawn into it with all my senses but knowing I am physically in my bed. I am not feeling any fear, resistance, panic. I am not feeling anything. I am just here. I have no sense of emotion or thought about the experience at all.

There is very little light coming through my bedroom window. The curtains are drawn, and even though there is a slight opening between them, allowing a thin slit of light to break up the darkness in the room, there is no way that this pool of living light could be possible from an outside light source.

I have no idea how long it has taken for the light spot to expand into the rippling light pool on the wall. I have no awareness of how long it was there before I was jolted awake to watch it. I have no sense of how long it has danced on the wall or how long it has taken to grow smaller and smaller and reduce itself back down into the golf ball light spot. I have no memory of the ball of light disappearing or what happened after that.

These terrifying nightly experiences regularly continued for the next five years. Some nights it was the sense of paralyzing numbness before the terror of the thick dark locust buzz-hum came down the hall into my room, and hovering for God knows how long near the ceiling in the corner. I played dead and prayed that whatever it was wouldn't hurt my family or me. I have no memory of time, how long it would be there, or what it wanted. I have no recollection of whether the buzz-hum and the light ball would show up on the same nights.

All I know is that I seemed to be the central focus of these bizarre and paralyzing terrors of the night and that no one else in my family was experiencing it. I also felt that if I stayed awake and kept the "focus" on me that it would keep the rest of my family safe. I didn't sleep for almost five years. I catnapped the nights away through those frightening years of my young childhood. When we moved from California to Ohio, it all stopped. For a while. Perhaps this was a precursor, the foundation, to who and what I was to become as I grew up.

I never told anyone about my terrors of the night. I was ten. Who would ever believe me?

CHAPTER 2

1988

Now let's move forward a few decades and roll right past those awkward high school years of zits, braces and hormones and "fitting in." And for God's sake, let's race past those pesky years of growing into young adulthood with a LOT of hormones, a sense of false invincibility covering up the insecurities and concerns about self-image and other peoples' opinions, obsessions about being "cool" and accepted, the need to have a boyfriend like everyone else or be considered "uncool," so you settle for a guy who isn't the most appropriate, blah, blah, blah. We've all been there. And then hopefully, from all of those experiences, we learn to make better choices and grow up.

I learned a LOT from those years. A lot of positive lessons, many very painful ones. But I learned, and I owned the responsibility for my role in experiences I created for myself. I was able to reflect on how my choices helped create the situations I put myself in...and I grew up. I am grateful for every moment of my life and all of the events and people I have experienced to become who I have become in this very moment. And I blame no one. So let's move on to how life started to unfold for me, beginning in early 1988.

I had been working as a flight attendant with Piedmont Airlines for a little over a year, based in Charlotte, NC, living in beautiful Clearwater, Florida. The airlines don't care where you live as long as you get to work, so I commuted up to Charlotte from Tampa for work. How did I end up in Clearwater? Well, I am drawn to the beach, the sun, white beaches, and it was there. I went down to "feel out" the area from St. Pete up to Clearwater and started checking out real estate. A couple of months later, I found a little beach cottage near the inter coastal in Clearwater and moved to Florida. Picking up and moving to a new city where I don't know anyone is no big deal to me even though it freaks most people out. I get an itch to relocate to a new place, visit it once or twice looking for real estate, find a place and buy it, pack up the pussycats and go. I generally let my folks know I am moving after I have moved. They keep my address in pencil in their address book. No biggie, they are used to it, and it gives the other family members something to talk about.

I love Clearwater and was enjoying my sun time, working out, reading everything I could get my hands on about metaphysical, "new age" and esoteric "stuff." I had developed a healthy appetite for those unseen forces in life, nature, as well as different philosophies on how these invisible forces work. Alternative healing modalities fascinated me, as did eastern philosophies that respect and readily accept the power of energies that can't be seen, yet are experienced with real life results.

I had a regular routine each day I was home in Clearwater. I would get up and head to Clearwater Beach early in the morning before the crowds showed up. I would tote my beach chair, towel, and latest reading material to the Palm Pavilion, where they guys at the breakfast bar had gotten used to my daily visits when I was in town. Seeing me coming from the parking lot, they would have my fried egg and cheese on wheat toast and coffee ready for me to pick up and eat in the pavilion before refilling my coffee and heading out to the beach for my day in the sun.

I would go out to the beach generally from 8:30 or 9:00 when it was still cool, and the white spun sugar sand had been freshly raked. Staying a couple of hours, I would leave before the high noon heat and when it got a wee bit noisy with tourists, wild kids, and mayhem that only being at the beach can offer.

I was lying there one morning in that cobwebby, hypnotic, out-of-body state we all fall into when we are at the beach. I drank in the chatter of the seagulls, the whisper of the waves gently rolling in and quietly sneaking back out again. The sun was showering down a delicious warmth that soaked to the bone, a light gulf breeze brushing me with a soft caress. The absolute perfection and contentment of being right there in that moment in time allows my mind to drift off and wander wherever it chooses to go. And then in an instant I was snapped out of that otherworldly serenity as if I had been hit with a bolt of lightning.

Even with the sounds and smells of nature and the beach were a soothing symphony playing around my very being, that portent of terror from my childhood, the vacuum-like silence that had possessed my young life, rolled over that safe comfort like a silent killer tsunami, tossing me back to a time I thought I had forgotten. I knew what was coming. I always did. Here it came. That familiar locust-like buzzing from my childhood came out of nowhere pervading the air around me, filling me to the bone. Where the hell had this distant terror from the past come from?! And why was it here now?

I physically jumped as my nerves reacted to the jolt, bringing me abruptly and rudely back into my body, a bit disoriented, a terrifying image in my head that I thought had been put to rest almost twenty-five years ago. My heart quickened, panic thumping in my chest like a cornered frightened bird, as I tried to escape from the familiar long-ago terror in my mind. There was nowhere to go but here.

This is all in my head. It isn't really happening. At least this is what I keep telling myself. I took a deep breath, exhaled, and from somewhere deep within my core, I knew without knowing that this flashback to the terrors of my childhood couldn't hurt me. This is different somehow. The same vacuum-like silence is manifesting just before the incessant buzzing that brought the terrors of the night. But this is different. I know I am okay. I'm at the beach in the safe warmth of the sun. I am okay.

I was quite content to be in this experience, lying in the luscious warmth of the sun in my familiar spot on my favorite beach. What seemed to peak my curiosity more than anything was that I wasn't freaking out over the freakiness of the situation. Now that's freaky. And there was so much more on its way.

As I lay there in wonderment at the shift in the air, I hear a woman's voice whispering in my ear saying, "I'm sorry." Just as real as anyone leaning down and speaking softly as if not to disturb me.

"I'm sorry." At the same instant I heard those words, a very clear image of my deceased mother, Marilyn, popped onto the mind screen in my head. What the hell?! I opened my eyes and looked around to see where the voice was coming from. No one was there.

My mother had died when I was a young girl. We weren't very close, and she was always ill with debilitating migraine headaches. I was young, second oldest with an older brother and two younger brothers, one just a year old. I never really felt a great sense of loss when Marilyn died. I know that sounds bizarre or that I was in denial, or I was just young and didn't understand what death was. It seemed like a life event that just happens. I wasn't attached one way or the other, being much more concerned with how Marilyn's passing was affecting my dad, and being a single father with four little kids. Looking back at that attitude many years later, it dawned on me that that was a pretty deep position to take as a small child. Perhaps it was a powerful foreshadowing of who I was to become and what I was to do in life. Marilyn's mother, my grandmother, had been living with us at the time of Marilyn's untimely death in the middle of the night. Because Marilyn was always so under the weather, "Gram" seemed more like a mom to the boys and I. Perhaps as a young girl, not understanding death, I detached from a sense of loss. Marilyn and I just weren't that close, I was okay with that, life went on, and I grew up.

It had been 25 years since Marilyn's death, and now she shows up in my head just as real as if she were in front of me, whispering in my ear. She looked good. She appeared to be in her early thirties, looked vibrant and healthy and full of life. Not only was she a vivid image on my mind screen, I audibly heard my deceased mother say "I'm sorry." And then just as quickly she was gone.

The sounds of the gulls and the gentle waves swam back up to the surface of my mind, dropping this amazing experience to drift just below the surface, not far away, waiting to be continued when it was time. I didn't have to wait long for the next installment of where this bizarre experience in the sun was going to take me as an adult. I knew without knowing that my life was going to become an action-packed adventure, and I wondered if I needed a helmet.

I wondered about this amazing experience but simply let it go to wherever experiences like this go, lulling back into beach mode, drinking in the rays and being blissfully content just to be right here right now. It was as if this were nothing out of the ordinary, completely natural, and a "normal" occurrence in life. Well, at least in my life it would prove to be normal. I was soon to discover that "normal" in my world would hardly fit the definition of normal for most folks. I was also soon to discover just how alive and full of life my deceased mother Marilyn was, what an amazing relationship we were going to have, and how, with her help, I would be able to help people in ways I couldn't even begin to imagine. But what was she sorry for?

I went to the beach the next morning with anticipation that Marilyn would show up again and that we could continue our brief encounter from the day before. I settled in with my egg and cheese sandwich and coffee and drifted into the energy of the sun and the sound of the waves. I didn't bring a book because I was focused on a visit from Marilyn. She never showed.

Day after day, each day that I wasn't flying, I would go to the beach, expecting to have Marilyn pop in again to at least say hello. And day after day she never showed. I know I hadn't imagined it. I HEARD her say, "I'm sorry." I SAW her in my mind just as real as if she were standing in front of me. Now I was getting pissed that she was doing this to me, wondering what the point of her showing up was in the first place. And then I just let go of the expectation of seeing her. It was just a fluke. Too much sun. Or too much mayo on my egg and cheese sandwich that day.

And that's when she showed up again. A few weeks later, I had settled on the sugary white sand, just finishing my breakfast sandwich and coffee. I had just started a fresh detective novel when the vacuum-like silence rolled over me, followed by the locust-buzz in my head. Something was going to happen, and I didn't have to wait long for the show to start. Interesting that now with the onset of the dead silence and the familiar buzzing, I was no longer frightened but looking forward to it. I was okay. I knew I was okay. Whatever was going to happen from now on was going to be a wonderful and life-changing adventure, and I was safe to explore life and all its many crevasses and dark places with childlike curiosity and open-hearted trust.

I put my book aside, stretched out on my back wrapped in the warmth of the sun, and allowed myself to simply drop into a state of nothingness, with an anticipation that something was going to happen without any expectation of what that something was going to be. A wave of expansive contentment rolled over me. And there she was. Marilyn, in all her vibrant energy, was with me again. Interestingly she wasn't an image on the mind screen in my head. She was standing right in front of me, just as solid as a human could be. Okay, she kind of "undulated" and looked a bit wavy. But she was solid. She had been dead for 25 years, and here she stood, full of life, vibrant, healthy, with a mischievous twinkle in her eyes. She reminded me of Dennis the menace just waiting to stir up some trouble. That can't be good.

Instead of audibly hearing her speak in my ear, Marilyn "thought-spoke" to me as clearly as if she were speaking out loud. She didn't move her lips, and no vocal cords were involved. It didn't take but a moment for me to realize that I could speak to her the same way, without embarrassing myself and having people look at me funny when they saw me talking out loud to the air. An interesting way of communicating that felt just as natural and real as human vocal cord conversation. "Thought-talk" was just one of many gifts I was going to soon embrace.

Marilyn told me once again that she was sorry. She didn't seem to be remorseful or full of regret or guilt. It was simply an unemotional acknowledgment of something from long ago. I asked her what she was sorry for, and she thought spoke, "You will know in time." What the hell was that supposed to mean? Apparently it was irrelevant for now as she brushed right over that and went off in another direction with the conversation. I was going to grow to really dislike hearing her saying "You will know in time." Smartass.

She went on to tell me that the reason that she hadn't shown back up at the beach was because I had gotten in my own way with my expectations and had blocked her from coming through. When we in the dimension of 3-D human have expectations or definite ideas of how things are supposed to be, it blocks those who have passed from coming through easily to communicate with us. The more we "let go" and allow ourselves to get out of our own way, the more we can experience other frequencies, dimensions, energy patterns and vibrations.

Choosing to allow ourselves to shift perceptions from the head and ego, dropping into the nothingness of all that is possible with open-hearted curiosity, opens up resonance to infinite potentials, magic and miracles on all levels. Drop your awareness into the nothingness of the void, trust and let go, and every moment is power. I'm getting a quantum physics lesson from my deceased mother. Great.

Marilyn explained that after our first encounter I had it in my head that I expected to see her again. Expectations always jam up the universal shifts of perception. We can experience multiple dimensions or frequencies at the same time by shifting our perception. I was all about being in my head, my ego at play with how I expected things to happen, and how Marilyn was SUPPOSED to show up. Apparently that isn't how to play with the universe.

Those that have passed are of a finer vibration, yet occupy the same space as we in 3-D. For them to get our attention, we have to shift our energies a bit to allow ourselves to perceive other dimensions with no preconceived notion of what they are. Being in the head is very thick stuff, very 3-D, very human, very egoist, very linear, very limiting. They cannot draw our attention into their finer vibration if we aren't paying attention. Makes sense.

Marilyn explained that there is no "other side." Whenever you embrace the concept that there is an "other side," your human perception automatically creates a sense of separation from our departed, a sense of unreachability and distance. Some of those who can communicate with the departed use the "other side" thing so much that we are conditioned to embracing a sense of separation from our loved ones...out of reach. The departed are not "out there" somewhere but right here with us in the same space. All dimensions are right here right now. Reality begins and ends with the perceiver, so if you SHIFT your perceptions, you SHIFT your reality.

Spirit communicators, however they sense that they are doing it, and regardless of whether they use the concept of "connecting with departed loved ones on the other side," are truly just allowing themselves to be open to the Divine in order to perceive other energies, frequencies, dimensions, patterns, vibrations that exist right here in the same space as 3-D.

Put some large rocks in a large jar and imagine that they represent you and other humans living in human 3-D. Now pour some rice over those rocks, covering them up completely. The little grains of rice move around and settle between the rocks. This can be perceived as those that have departed, died, transitioned out of 3-D physicality. Rocks and rice are occupying the same space at the same time. Play some more and add sand to the jar. Another finer dimension is occupying the same space. Add some water and perceive yet another higher frequency and dimension. You can keep going with breaking down the water molecules into hydrogen and oxygen, and break that down even more into atoms, and on and on.

Marilyn explained to me that the key to being "dimensionless," embracing the totality of nothingness, is in the letting go of what we have been conditioned to believe as "real." This in turn opens us up to the Divine and infinite possibilities. Physical death is an illusion and part of the illusion of duality that we 3-D'ers get stuck in. Life/death, black/white, good/bad. We have allowed ourselves to be mummified in 3D conditioning, into the concept of limitation and false reality. When we open to Divine with trust, we can receive and transmit huge amounts of energy, light and information from many dimensions without effort.

Allow yourself to simply trust in the God of your understanding, the Divine, dropping into that space of expansive nothingness, bliss, expanded awareness. This divine nothingness is the pure truth of our natural power to manifest, create, and BE the perfection of the universe. By simply choosing to drop into this nothingness of divine bliss, all is possible. Our loved ones and pets that have "died," are all very much alive and well and would love to communicate with us. The thickness of 3-D, our humanness and how we choose to live, how we have been conditioned to believe. This is the smothering mummy wrapping that is keeping us from infinite potential and possibility.

Physics tells us that energy is never destroyed. It just changes form. Time, distance and space don't exist. I guess I am allowing myself to "shift" perceptions to embrace this weirdness. After all, I am at the beach in Clearwater, Florida, having a very interesting "chat" with my mother, Marilyn, who has been "dead" for 25 years, but in reality, is very much alive and well and educating me about physics. Not that any of it makes any sense to me at this point, but it is still very cool.

Marilyn looked at me calmly and thought-spoke, "Now that you have allowed yourself to open to Divine, different realities, and you are loosening the pattern of your humanness a bit, you are going to start your fantastic journey as a helper, a healer, a guide, a guardian, a watcher, and a teacher. I will help you along for a while until you embrace these talents fully, and until you let the training wheels of doubt spin off, and you fly free with confidence and power, serving Divine as best you can."

And then she was gone. Blinked out. Poof. I was left with more questions than answers. I thought-spoke a question to the space that she had just occupied, asking what I do now. An otherworldly impish chuckle came back with, "You'll know in time." Smart-aleck.

Somehow this whole experience seemed quite natural, as if I had just taken a step in my "evolvement" into whatever or whoever I was to become in life. At this moment, I felt calm, serene, trusting, with a childlike sense of curiosity, looking forward to the adventure. Oddly, I also had a feeling that this was somehow familiar, that I was beginning to remember things about my purpose in life. I dropped into that hypnotic ripple of sun, sand, waves and nothingness, perfectly to just BE, attached to absolutely nothing. Not even the moment.

I commuted to Charlotte from Tampa the next morning, heading off on a four-day trip, overnighting three nights in a different city each night, probably in different time zones. It was on this particular trip that I was made aware of the first "gift" I would accept on this journey.

I was flying with a flight attendant that I had known for a couple of years, and we both got to the airplane before the rest of the crew arrived for the beginning of the trip. As I was chatting with her, catching up on what she had been doing, I noticed a tall man standing behind her. The man looked "real" and solid except that he was a bit "wavy" as Marilyn had been at the beach. Somehow I knew that he was from that dimension that occupies space within our space; the rice between the rocks in the jar that Marilyn had described to me on the beach. I knew without knowing, questioning or even doubting, that this was the spirit of someone who had "died" and was associated with my fellow flight attendant standing in front of me. Super. What the heck am I supposed to do with that? Keep in mind that this little adventure was taking place way before mediums and spirit communicators were popular, all over TV with their reality shows. Marilyn hadn't told me what was going to happen or what to do with whatever it is that I was going to start "receiving." Apparently there are no instruction manuals that come with these intuitive gifts and you "adjust" as you go. Now would probably be a good time for that helmet.

When I asked my fellow flight attendant how she had been doing, she said that she was doing okay, still recovering from her stepfather's death a few weeks ago. She went on to say that he had been more like a father to her than her own father, and even though his passing had not been a surprise, it was still hard for her to get over.

And then I just started talking. I allowed my attention to stay with the dimensionless energy of the gentleman. I began to speak, based on what can be best described as "ripples" or patterns of information and energy that I was picking up. He was sending vibrational information to me that I was somehow able to receive, translate into 3-D, and transmit to my friend in a way that would be most appropriate for her, and easy for her to comprehend.

Somehow I knew from the rippling information he sent me that he had died from some sort of interference in the pattern of the chest area. I then sensed that it was a lung issue. Then he thought-talked to me with things he would like me to pass on to his stepdaughter. Okie Dokie. Let's see how this plays out.

I jumped right in with both feet and asked her if her stepdad had passed from some illness having to do with the chest area or his lungs. She was startled at the question and asked how I knew that. Too late to pull anything back, so I forged ahead as the information I received came out of my mouth much more quickly than my brain could have made it up. There is no thinking with this stuff. The information coming from dimensionless reality seems to fly out of my mouth at a rapid pace, so it's quite obvious that I haven't had time to think it up. Thinking isn't part of the program. Offering healing energy and information to people is the gift. AND, because I am just the mouthpiece and the messenger, I don't remember anything I tell people. It's none of my business. Just the messenger. I also have no attachment to how you take what I tell you or what you do with it. It's none of my business. I care if I have served you well. Don't care so much about what you do with it all. But I digress.

My flight attendant friend confirmed that her stepdad had died from lung cancer. He had me tell her that it was a quiet and peaceful passing, no struggle or discomfort, and that now he was breathing in life fully. He was completely regenerated, rejuvenated, his DNA and RNA re-patterned and restored to the vibration, energy and light of the dimensionless reality where he is healthy and renewed.

She was shocked and dumbfounded at what I told her, but she didn't lose it and start crying until I mentioned that it was his wish that she have his walking stick. I had no idea what this was about. I was just passing on the information. I described a beautiful walking stick that had some unique carving on the knob. How would I know this if he weren't showing me?

Through her tears, she told me of a beautiful walking stick he had gotten from his grandfather that she had always loved. Before his passing, as she was sitting with him between visits from hospice personnel, he told her that he wanted her to have it and to take it with her after their visit. She took it when she left. He died later that night.

So now I have my co-worker sobbing like a baby with relief that her step-dad was okay and full of life, feeling great love for him, and a gratitude for life that she had forgotten that she had. Little did I know at this moment that over the coming years, I would make hundreds of people cry. I would grow to LOVE making people cry with relief, joy, closure, wrapped in the concept that we "survive" the illusion of physical death. When we shift our perceptions, we shift our reality. Open ourselves to Divine, let go and trust, and worlds upon worlds of potential open up. We receive what we open ourselves to.

It was at this moment of great release for the flight attendant that the rest of the crew came on board the plane for our pre-trip crew briefing. And as she excitedly explained the gift I had just given her through her tears of joy, acceptance, and final release of her grief, my reputation as a medium, spirit communicator, "flight-attendant-who-sees-dead-people" was born. Little did I know at that time that it would be just one of many gifts that I would be blessed with over the years to offer people comfort and healing. The train of my true mission in life had left the station, and it would prove to be quite a ride. Sometimes very uncomfortable, and challenging for me, a bit too weird and "scary" for most people, (who would pray for my black soul as they accused me of doing things with Satan that I wasn't even doing with a live guy), my life of unique service to others was becoming my greatest passion. My life was becoming my greatest gift...to me.

CHAPTER 3

Let the Games Begin

And so it was that after my reunion with Marilyn on the beach, I began developing and embracing some pretty unique gifts. The first of these gifts was my ability to perceive and communicate with departed loved ones and pets. This new ability began manifesting itself on the very next trip I worked after reuniting with Marilyn. I was chatting with Kim, one of the flight attendants I was working this trip with, during a break between flights. We had an hour before boarding the next leg of the day, and while we sat there, I "saw" a tall, slim man standing behind Kim, smiling. He was as real as Kim was. He was solid, yet I knew he was a spirit. I got a sense of his personality, how he was feeling physically, and that he was glad I was there to intercede for him. I knew without knowing that he was Kim's father. Even though I had never flown with her before, didn't know her in any way, I had the ability to connect these two who had been so close in life. Now, how do I do this without sending Kim screaming off the plane and me being taken off the trip for a psych evaluation?

This was my virgin voyage into the realm of the other side, I had big training wheels on this bike into the unknown, and serious performance anxiety going on. I sent a quick SOS out to the universe, asking that I say what was most appropriate, and that I handle the situation according to what serves both Kim and her father the best.

I took a deep breath, exhaled, focused on my intention, sidestepped all doubt, inadequacy, and what Kim may think. I set my intent for service to Kim, let go, dropped into the space of divine resonance, and allowed the universe to take over.

After dropping down, I instantly felt very empowered, confident, and knew I was doing some amazing and unique healing work here. Almost as if I was shifting into a different "me," I had no doubt that Kim would be given a tremendous blessing with this "reading." She and her dad would have a memorable moment through me as their connector.

During a break in the conversation, I asked Kim if she had recently lost a male close to her. I got the impression of "father" or father figure to her who had passed within the last year or so. With a deer-in-the-headlights look on her face, and tears forming in her eyes, she told me that her father had passed ten months ago, and she missed him terribly.

I was sensing, not thinking, and began speaking very quickly with no idea what I was saying. I told Kim to pay close attention to what I was saying because I am just the messenger delivering a note of sorts from other dimensions. The message was none of my business, and I would not remember or "store" the information I was passing on to her. It was amazing that she didn't react as if I was some freak or thought that I was crazy. She didn't seem frightened in any way. She seemed fascinated, and since this was my first communication from the other side other than Marilyn, I was just as fascinated.

I described a man that stood behind Kim's left shoulder, with the sense that this was indeed her dad. Also, he was very much alive and well, and he loved her very much. This brought tears and a huge feeling of relief for Kim, but in my mind, I felt I had told her what any carnival fortune teller could have told her. I was the disbeliever here. This soon passed as the experience continued.

Dad wanted to have me tell Kim that his lungs were much better now. He was deeply inhaling fresh air, breathing in the amazing fullness of life, he was happy, doing well, and he loved her very much. In that instant, I got a flash of an old black and white photo, with a tall, slender man standing next to a heavier woman who was sitting ramrod straight in a high-backed chair. Her hands were resting on the top of an intricately carved thick wooden cane in front of her. The photo looked like it was taken in the late 1800's when you looked very serious, and no one smiled. He looked miserably uncomfortable, his collar looked too tight, and I got the impression that this dressing up stuff, posing for a camera, just wasn't his cup of tea. The woman with the cane looked quite stern, with no apparent sense of humor, had a tight bun and a wee trace of a mustache on her upper lip. I also got the impression that this was a husband and wife; she was the one who wore the pants in the family and was a living definition of a true matriarch. Mama ran the family with a firm hand and a really big stick.

I relayed what I was seeing to Kim, and she shook her head, not knowing who these people were, moved to tears that her dad was here. She asked me what else I saw. I took this as a good sign, and with my confidence boosted, I continued. Her dad was still there and wanted me to pass on that these folks were her mother's parents. He brought them through as a gift for her mom and confirmation that we survive physical death. My attention was drawn to the wooden cane the woman had in front of her. Almost as if my perception was zooming in, I was able to see the fantastic workmanship and painstaking detail of the piece. It looked like it was carved from a single piece of rich mahogany wood, with a flourish of intricate flowers and leaves, snaking around the cane from top to bottom. The very top of the cane was a thick knob carved into the shape of a hand, delicate fingers curved over the rounded top to be the handhold for the user. There was a small red oval crystal of some kind encrusted in an exquisite ring design carved into the wood on the ring finger of the hand.

It was a beautiful cane, a one-of-a-kind piece, and I knew it had been carved specifically for this powerful matriarch. I passed all of this on to Kim speaking quickly, as if I was in a hurry to get it out. This isn't because I had to tell her while I remembered what was in my mind. My mind wasn't involved at all. The images and my perceptions were coming too quickly for my left brain to wrap itself around. This was a good sign that my brain didn't have time to think this stuff up, process it, and then verbalize it. I was just talking too fast and knew that the information I was passing on came from a place outside of my brain. I definitely was not in my head and the 3D of human thought.

In a heartbeat, I had set my focus to serve Kim and her father, put the intention on my clipboard, and let go of it. I trusted the universe to provide me with the information and appropriate words for the situation. I continued to ramble on with all the information I was receiving so quickly from "wherever." She listened to me with fascination when I spoke of the matriarch telling me that she had been mean-spirited and not well-liked while in her skin suit here on our side. She learned a lot about how she treated people while she was experiencing her life review at the moment of death, her life passing in front of her eyes. She was able to see and sense how people had experienced her while she was alive, how her actions created the reactions of friends and loved ones, creating, and sometimes destroying the relationships that she had.

She wanted Kim to know that she had died before anyone knew about bipolar disorder and manic depression, and for the most part, she just didn't feel good most of her life. Her life had been a roller coaster of emotions that terrified her at times, feeling off balance and not centered for most of her life. She was never deemed crazy, thank God. Back in that day, the "treatment" would have been horrific, incredibly cruel, and would have driven her over the edge for sure.

The matriarch, through her life review, was able to comprehend, understand and accept all of this without thought, opinion or judgment. It was an uncomfortable, yet loving experience that offered the contrast between living in the tightness of fear, ego, and the dark emotions, and living from a space of expansiveness, light and love. After her life passed in front of her eyes, and she had shifted into 4D vibration, she had gently been asked by "guides" what she had learned from her human experience and her life review.

She wanted me to tell Kim that love is a state of being, not a verb, not a noun; a state of sensing and feeling, not thought and feelings. Thinking gets you nowhere but into a lot of trouble, serving no one and poisoning everyone's life, especially your own. She was no longer mean-spirited, angry or full of fear. Most of her life she just had not felt well. She was feeling fine now, learning a lot, and there were many souls there she was reconnecting with, as well as new ones she resonated with. She no longer needed the cane. Kim said that she had never met her grandparents; they both had died before she was born. The matriarch began waving her cane around and wanted me to have Kim remind her own mother of it and how she had acquired it. Kim's father wanted me to make sure that she remembered him to her mom. He emphasized that the love lives on, he was glad that he was able to come through, bringing Kim's mom, the love of his life, the best gift he could think of; a visit from her mother's own parents.

They all began to fade out, indicating that my first amazing experience as a spirit medium was closing. It was remarkable that doing this felt as natural to me as breathing. Kim was very receptive to what I was telling her, thanking me for easing her sense of loss and giving her the knowing that our loved ones who have passed are alive and well. She believed they had really been there. I knew too many details to be making anything up. Even though she never knew her grandparents, she would be calling her mom that night and would tell her all about the visit.

The next morning after our layover in Chicago, Kim sat next to me on the hotel van and told me she had spoken with her mom last night after we had gotten to the hotel. Mom began crying almost immediately when Kim told her about her dad and how much he still loves her. She completely broke down when Kim told her that her dad had brought through her own parents as a gift to her. Kim described them in detail, including the beautifully carved mahogany cane with the oval red crystal inlaid in the etched ring on the delicate wooden hand at the top.

Mom had suddenly gotten silent and Kim got concerned. After several seconds, she heard mom take a deep breath, exhale and sob a bit more. Then she told Kim that she had known her entire life that her mom was genuinely a very loving woman; she just didn't know how to show it. She knew both of her parents loved her dearly and now was convinced because of what I had seen and told Kim. Kim's parents had worked hard their entire lives, they didn't have a lot of money, and life was hard on a farm in the Midwest. When the matriarch, Kim's grandmother got severe arthritis in her hip at a very young age, it was difficult for her to walk, let alone help around the place. This was frustrating to her, and she became more depressed and mean. Then she found out that she was pregnant and, even though she was thrilled with the news, the hormonal roller coaster sent her into a deeper funk.

Kim's mom had told her that her grandfather had begun carving a magnificent cane for his wife while sitting with her, talking to her gently and quietly, easing some of her discomfort while he carved the exquisite design in the wood.

Riding in the hotel van, I received more information to pass on to Kim as I said, "Your mother was born just as he was finishing the piece. She was such a beautiful sweet baby, born with an amazing sense of calm that soothed your grandmother even more, easing her agonizing bouts of up-and-down emotional swings."

On a roll now with my perceptions lighting up like July 4th fireworks, I added, "Your grandfather was finishing work on the cane when your mother was born. That's when he chose to inlay the ruby crystal in the ring on the wooden finger at the top of your grandmother's cane. Born in July, your mother was a cherished blessing to both of them. The birthstone for July is the ruby, and Ruby is what they named their precious daughter, your mother."

With this information, Kim was completely blown away. I had not only connected her with her dad; I was able to connect her to her deceased grandparents whom she had never met and had no knowledge of. I was able to put a name correctly to her mother with the correct birth month. My life was becoming curiouser and curiouser by the day.

As the months went on, I began having a lot of practice connecting deceased loved ones and pets with coworkers. A couple of flight attendants may be in the back galley after our cabin service when we have time to chat. Either some deceased spirit pops in, and I can tell psychically who they go to, or a flight attendant will mention that they have lost someone recently. The deceased person or pet comes through at the instant the flight attendant begins to speak about it. I am just open to Source with trust that I will be an appropriate conduit for whatever would serve them for the highest good.

I amaze even myself with the things I told them, the messages given from beyond with so much love. There is no way I could be so detailed about certain things if the deceased weren't right there giving me the information. Many times, like with Kim, I give people information that they would have no knowledge of, yet when they talk to another surviving family member or friend, the information is confirmed as accurate.

It didn't take long for me to begin to love doing this work, especially when I can make everyone cry. The tears are always of relief, release, closure, forgiveness, or simply the peace in knowing their loved ones are alive and well on the other side.

Let me take a moment here and describe the gifts I began embracing and opening up to. When I "see" departed loved ones they are as physically real to me as looking at someone in person. If you close your eyes and visualize your mom or dad in your mind, are they not as real to you as if they were right there with you or as a living photograph in your head? That's how I "see" people. Clairvoyance—clear sight. When I "hear" a person to get information, it's like telepathy or someone speaking to me from the outside of my head. Voices or messages, the ESP or telepathy that I can tap into is known as clairaudience—clear hearing. If someone tells you that they hear voices coming from inside their head, I suggest that you run really fast in the opposite direction. Believe me, there is only room for one of me in my skull. I don't like crowds.

"But what if it's my angels or guides talking to me?" you ask. Your angels and guides will come in through your heart-space, not the ego attic in your head. This is that still small voice of Spirit mentioned in the Bible. Your true heart and the heart of Source, the Creator, God, Universal Mind...whatever the God of your understanding is. If it comes from the neck up, and it is loud, it is NOT spirit.

Sometimes I don't see anything visually or hear anything auditorily, or get any telepathic messages from anyone. I may just get a "sense" of some emotion or feeling from the deceased. These perceptions come from my gut and is known as clairsentience—clear sensing. Sometimes I simply know without knowing. This too comes from the infinite heart space, the gut, and is known as claircognizance.

I use whatever tools Source offers me on a case-by-case, person-by-person basis. I know where these gifts come from, and where it comes from is far greater than 3D and my "humanness." Whatever comes through, however that may be or as bizarre as it may seem, is being delivered through me from the Creator...and I trust it.

All I do as the conveyor of information is to set my intent to get out of the way, become a conduit, portal or a magnifier, to optimize the client's energy through the grace of the god of their understanding.

It doesn't matter to me how people perceive "God." I shift into multi-dimensionality where there are no labels, definitions or duality. **SOELI** (**S**ource **O**f **E**nergy - **L**ight - **I**nformation) is my constant companion and pretty much sums up all of the labels and definitions of the divine that I can imagine. Call your god whatever you like. **SOELI** is the universal energy that can handle all of the labels and definitions you want to attach to that which is greater than we are. Everything is made up of all the same "stuff" regardless of your perceptions. We are all a bit of the stardust of **SOELI**. Pure energy, light and information with opinions, judgments and beliefs wrapped tightly around that wee bit of stardust, forming our lives, sometimes choking ourselves to death in the smog of 3D. I think I will stay the wee bit of stardust and play "out there" as much as possible.

At the end of the day, after I have worked with a client, I ask myself two simple questions. Did I use all my gifts as best I could with this person? Yes. Did I do or cause any harm? No.

The first question I must be able to answer "Yes." The second I had better be able to answer honestly "No." If I can do this, I've had a very big day. Win-win for everyone.

CHAPTER 4

"Being" Psychic

This may be a good time for me to describe how we are all "psychic," how we can choose (or not choose) to utilize whatever natural, intuitive gifts that are woven into our energy patterns before we are born. We come into this life with all the gifts that Source has to offer. How we are conditioned, how we believe, what we perceive; this creates our reality, molding our 3D lives. Your choices are what make you who you are. You may or may not embrace your fine-tuned innate intuitive abilities. And whatever you choose is okay. Some people embrace one or two, some don't want to "have" any of these gifts, and some (like me) jump on the magic carpet and say, "let's play!"

"God" doesn't care whether you use any of them or not. They are part of the fabric that is you. If your journey involves using any of these gifts, you will. If you choose NOT to even believe that being psychic is part of your natural legacy, you fear it, believing it is "devil stuff," that's okay also. Your journey. Your path. Your soul. I'm simply giving you a bit of information you may not have about some of the gifts you may not know about. If anything resonates with you, follow your curiosity. Research. Investigate. Explore.

There are many flavors of being "psychic." Layers and layers of sensitivities and senses. We have the basic five physical senses of hearing, seeing, smelling, taste and touch that we rely on as part of our physical existence. Most of the "senses" we use to send and receive information to the brain can be quite subtle and are too numerous to talk about. The sense of danger. The sense of temperature in the air. We don't pay much attention to our sense of space, movement. You can't touch your finger to your nose, even with your eyes closed, without a sense of space or movement. Climbing stairs would be impossible. We wouldn't survive without our hundreds of senses, whether they be subtle or more obvious. The easiest way to define a "sense" is that senses are channels between your brain and your body to send and receive information to "sense" your body's **relation** to the outside world in order to **experience** the outside world.

There are many "clair" (clear) senses that are associated with "being psychic." Too many to list here, I am offering information on the ones that have become great tools for me and my work.

"Clairaudience" is the ability to "hear" information. This is the way one can reveive messages from Source, loved ones (whether alive or passed on), other energies and spirits getting through to you through your psychic hearing. WARNING: If someone says they have voices coming from **inside** their head telling them to give you a message, RUN!!! That is a sign that they may have a brain problem, chemical imbalance or mental illness that is causing this. To me clairaudience is like hearing a message passing *through*, not *from*.

"Clairvoyance" - clear **"sight"** is the ability to "see" information and images in your mind's eye. What you are seeing isn't thought. It is simply images, perhaps a psychic video clip of an experience that you have no knowledge about or 3D experience with.

"Claircognizance" - clear **"knowing"** is the ability to know without knowing. Gut feeling with absolute certainty that you can't argue with. You don't know how you know. You just do. Trust that. I have found that trusting the soft subtlety of this is ALWAYs accurate.

"Clairsentience" - clear **"sensing"** is the ability to "pay attention" to what you sense or feel. Understand that psychic "sensing" and "feeling" have nothing to do with emotions or "feelings", even though by using this perceptive gift, you are able to sense "feelings" by simply "feeling" the energies and information you receive.

I have discovered something quite interesting over the many years of doing spirit communication work, connecting with the departed, as well as those that are "on their way" home at the edge of the physical horizon.

We ALL experience a life review, where we are able to get a quick glimpse of our lives; that "life passing in front of your eyes" we hear about. There is no judgement with this review. It is simply an exercise in awareness; an education of the small details in life that we never paid attention to. Remembering what WAS so we can let go and become more present with our true divine nature. Source.

I firmly feel that we are born with full psychic abilities, whether we acknowledge or use them in life. As we are passing from physicality to the "in-between," we begin to "remember" through our 3D life experiences, what we seemed to have forgotten about our divine natures and powerful abilities.

The first psychic gift that we seem to "remember" is clairsentience. As we zip through the tunnel, what I see kind of like a "slinky" of circular, spiralling time (time is not linear in my world), we get to "feel" and "sense" in the gut area, the "emotions" and "feelings" of those we leave behind. We are able to almost physically sense how our actions (or lack of action) made others feel emotionally, mentally, psychologically, even physically. This can be a very powerful experience as we go through the life review, clueless as to how we may have affected others with our choices, either hurtfully or with love and heart. Small acts of unconscious kindness as well as hurtful acts or words are presented. We simply acknowledge all this as information, not a judgment of any kind.

I have dealt with many of the departed that have committed suicide. How I sense their life review is that the slinky of time has been stretched out a bit, making their life review a bit longer (if "time" existed) and they are even more clairsentient than others. They are able to experience what their act did to the loved ones left behind; the emotions more "raw" so they really "get" how their act of taking their own life affected those left behind. Suicides are VERY aware of the remaining guilt, confusion, grief, pain, the "what could I have done to prevent this" that those left behind live with.

Again, there is absolutely no judgement with this. It is simply receiving pure "in-the-face" information for them to take to the in-between to learn from. Even though it may take a bit longer to get through the slinky, PLEASE be assured that suicides don't get stuck or go to "hell." Their life reviews are more powerful perhaps, however they do make it to the end of the slinky and the "lightness" of the in-between. You will know them again. **Everyone** will meet in that timeless state of grace of the in-between.

A suicide's clairsentience comes back quickly, profoundly and powerfully in their life review in order for them to learn as part of their soul's growth and evolvement. And who is to say that their act of suicide isn't part of YOUR journey; that they are in fact teachers offering you the opportunity to forgive, let go of the need to "understand" (which is the need of our egos, not spirit), make different choices, change your life to love better while you are here? Their act is your lesson to choose to pay attention and BE present right here right now. All you have is this moment. Choose carefully. Live more fully. The suicide souls are just fine. They may discover in their review that they in fact WERE here to leave just the way they did in order to teach those left behind. What a gift for them to comprehend that on their journey home. This is my experience with suicides and information I have received from them. Other perceptions are other perceptions...and are also okay. Whatever you believe - IS.

Go with what you get.

CHAPTER 5

Dilger, PA

I bought a tiny house in downtown Dilger (a fictitious name to protect the folks in the real town) and settled in with my small herd of pussycats, loving the people, the beautiful surroundings, and the simple life I had been craving. I was cautious at first about letting anyone know anything more about me than that I was a flight attendant based in Pittsburgh, desiring to live a quiet life in the forest. I don't remember how the information of my unique gifts came out, but I was very pleasantly surprised that all that I do, from communicating with the departed, the ghost hunting, and all the other "psychic" stuff, was not only accepted but very much embraced by a large percentage of folks. A few of them would go ghosting with me in the cemeteries to hook up with Grandma. I was asked about psychic stuff, as well as communicating with the departed while having coffee and a slice of Betty's award-winning pie up at Betty's Cafe. Betty's was the heart of Dilger and the go-to place for news and the gathering place for anything and everything going on in the area. Within a short walking distance from my house, I practically lived at Betty's, my place to socialize whenever I was in town. Sadly, Betty passed away, and the cafe is gone. Both are missed.

Little did I know how important Dilger would be in the development of new gifts and the expansion of the gifts I had at the time. The school of Dilger would be a portal of experience that would serve me to serve others on some pretty powerful and indescribable levels. This book is the first time I have opened up about a couple of difficult, bizarre and life-changing events that have brought me to this point in my life. I am grateful that I had these experiences in such a peaceful, serene and beautiful environment where I felt at home...safe.

My first three books were written and published while living in Dilger. Based in Pittsburgh, I would drive the two hours to the airport to go to work. When my seniority dropped a weensy bit, and I was getting some dog trips, I transferred to Philadelphia where I could fly more desirable trips, generally driving through the magnificent Cook's Forest to the little airport in Dubois, PA, to fly a commuter to PIT and then jet over to PHL. I was flying international flights out of Philly in 2003, and would always bring some goodies back from some European city to share with everyone who came into Betty's for early breakfast the day after I got back.

The girls who worked at the cafe learned how to read city codes, knew my schedule, and would send out the clarion call with what foreign city I was returning from. We would have a pretty good crowd at Betty's at 5:30 in the morning the day after my return.

The funniest episode was when I brought back some spotted dick with clotted cream from England. (Research it). The big tough guys sitting at the counter were a bit reluctant to try it. Since none of them wanted to be considered a wuss, they all manned up, picked up their spoons, and took a big spoonful as Betty passed the container down the counter. And then they asked for more. Hysterical.

Dilger was also where I began to fine-tune my communication abilities with the departed, which began to expand into the ability to communicate clearly with people on life support, in a coma, or actively dying and non-responsive. I began to be able to shift my perception enough to do this from any distance. I didn't have to be anywhere near people to be able to sense, feel and perceive very clearly what was going on around them and their loved ones, what they had to say, and exactly what they were experiencing at that moment. Time, distance and space have nothing to do with the patterns of energy, light and information being transmitted. I was as able to perceive as easily as if someone were right in front of me.

Most of the time, as soon as someone even begins talking about a person or pet that has passed or is very ill and dying, that person's energy comes through instantly, clearly and profoundly.

The folks in Dilger, population at that time, 497, were used to me and my quirky gifts, some had gone ghosting with me, and many had had great conversations with their departed through me. Most of the folks in town were very protective of me and my solitude, and I loved the security it afforded me.

I have realized that this gift of being able to transcend time, distance, space, as well as consciousness, is a powerful and profound way for me to immediately and sharply perceive several dimensions simultaneously in order to serve and heal. There is no attachment to the moment, no emotions, no thoughts, feelings or expectations of what the outcome or result should be.

Pure information, light, energy flashes through at an incredible vibration, frequency, and speed. The only way I can describe it is faster than the speed of light. In a nanosecond I "drop" into the moment, into the overlapping patterns of energy presented to me to become dimensionless, trusting that whatever I perceive will serve others to the best of my abilities and harm no one.

When these guys find out that I am available to be their mouthpiece, they get real excited, real chatty, thought-talk flying at blinding speed. Sometimes I have to ask them to slow down as I have to translate into human and use my vocal chords to deliver the messages. After all, we mere mortals are still fully mummified in 3D and a bit slow.

It didn't take long for people in the tiny village of Dilger to find out that I was also a paranormal investigator, a "ghost hunter." There are a couple of cemeteries there that never disappointed when I took folks out to hunt, everyone always having a personal experience or capturing some kind of photographic evidence that spirits were there.

I would go up to Betty's for breakfast after a cemetery investigation the night before, and one of the waitresses who lived across the road from Dilger Cemetery, would ask if I had been out at the cemetery the night before. I would tell her that I had been out with a couple of people, and she would say, "Thought so. I saw the red laser of the thermal scanner moving around over there and figured it was you." And where else but at Betty's Cafe could I learn how to gut a moose from one of the locals over a big thick cheeseburger? I love Dilger.

CHAPTER 6

The Dashun Ferry

I was sound asleep when I felt a light "tapping" on my shoulder, bringing me to just below the surface of a twilight sleep. I somehow knew without knowing that it was my mother, Marilyn. She wanted something. In the middle of the night. How rude. In a state of cobwebby drowsiness, I asked her what she wanted and couldn't this wait until morning.

"We have work to do, and you need to wake up a bit more to receive the assignment," she says.

What the heck was she talking about? Assignment? What assignment and why in the middle of the night?

"Just come to the surface for the assignment and then you can drop back into dream-time to task the job." What was she talking about? "Tasking" the job?

Marilyn continued her gentle badgering with an explanation. "You have an opportunity to take a quantum leap at this time, to expand your perception for service to others. With the acceptance of this ability, you will be able to be present in even more dimensions simultaneously, perceiving multiple vibrations, energies and patterns at the same time. You will have a clear knowing of which energy pattern to shift to that will be of the greatest service and highest good in that moment.

Since this is your first opportunity to experience this new shift of perception, you can task the job during your dream-time, clearly and lucidly, not expending much conscious energy, waking up rested in the morning."

Now, even though I sleep like the dead (pun intended) and wake up quickly with an obnoxious amount of high energy, it was around 2:30 in the morning, I had been smack in the middle of delicious deep sleep. I really didn't want to wake up right now. However, Marilyn was not going to leave this "assignment" thing alone. Having had a couple of years with Marilyn's "tapping" every now and then when it came to communicating with the departed, knowing that it always turned out with a lot of healing on many levels for many people, I began to pay attention through the haze of sleep.

Knowing that she had my attention, Marilyn continued, "You know you always have a choice as to what to accept and what not to accept, and that Divine will never give you anything that you can't handle. This is a tremendous opportunity for your soul growth as well as the opening of a portal of great healing for others. Simply acknowledge the assignment and you can begin to task the job at hand. It is urgent that you acknowledge and accept NOW."

"Okay, okay, I acknowledge that I was rudely woken up in the middle of the night by my not-so-alive-in-3D mother to accept some urgent assignment and task a job NOW, whatever the heck that means. Now what?" I asked.

"You'll know in time," she quietly responded, disappearing before I could call her a potty name. Man, I hate when she does that. I was instantly asleep, falling even more deeply asleep, and proceeded to have a very vivid and clear dream.

In the dream, my awareness was hovering as if an observer, above a very rugged and choppy sea sometime during daylight hours. I got the sense of frigid angry gray water, black sky, no shoreline to be seen. I am about fifteen feet off the surface in darkness, a churning stormy sea beneath me, and there are people in the water. Many people. And they were drowning. I had no emotions or feelings at this time. I was simply paying attention to what was going on, fine-tuning my awareness like a camera focuses on its field of view. I took it all in instantly as I expanded my vision, taking in the capsized boat, dead bodies floating in the violent, icy water, others still with life in them bobbing and crying and struggling hopelessly against the power of the turbulent freezing water that was sucking the life out of them. I saw so many without life vests sinking below the surface as if they were being pulled under by some invisible force, giving themselves up to the sea. There were others who had apparently had time to don life vests but had succumbed to hypothermia in the freezing water, their faces looking a strange bluish-white yet almost peaceful as they bobbed on the high gray waves.

I was witnessing the horrible deaths of dozens of people as they drowned in the turbid sea, as I seemed to "hover" 15-20 feet off the surface. I was feeling no emotion, no attachment to the tragedy unfolding before my eyes, yet I was feeling an expansive sense of compassion, an open-hearted desire to serve and help in whatever way I could. I was wrapped in a calm, powerful compassion for these souls that was far beyond anything human. I wasn't just wrapped in this compassion. I WAS this compassion. There are no words to describe this.

Over the next several minutes, I was drawn to one person and then another, getting close to them and hovering just a few feet away from and above them. Somehow they would "see" me and focus their dying eyes on however it was I was being projected to them. They would look directly at me for a moment with what appeared to be a look of curiosity. Then they radiated a look of gratitude, love, and grace as they quit struggling with the sea. An overwhelming sense of peace, calm and release embraced them, each face looking like a sweet child dropping innocently off to sleep in your arms. And they died.

One by one I drifted from one soul to another, being "present" with each drowning or freezing victim, holding the light for them at the moment of their passing and soul release, easing them with love and peace. I felt none of the physical sensations my charges felt. I was just "there." I felt only great compassion with detached awareness. There were no emotions or thinking. I knew it was important for me to hold the light and the portal open to help these souls have a smooth passing and release from everything 3D and "human." I helped 37 souls. What was interesting is that each soul, at the instant of their release, told me that they were grateful for me because no one would come looking for them. They thanked me for acknowledging them and their presence there. What did that mean...that no one would come looking for them?

There were dozens and dozens of victims in the water. I noticed that there were others out there like me hovering around and clearing souls. They all looked like beautiful shiny iridescent orbs of light. I observed them moving amongst the drowning just as I was, hovering just above the next victim about to take their last breath and release their soul, having a knowingness of the timing of the soul release for each. The orbs of light all appeared to be an opalescent transparent "shimmer" of unearthly colored light about four feet in diameter. They knew who their assignments were. They effectively and smoothly moved to each one when it was time, enveloping each of their charges in the most magnificent and indescribable radiance of pure love, light, and otherworldly protection, easing them out of discomfort, pain and fear, and into a peaceful release as they let go their struggle with 3D. I was a part of this. It felt familiar. I had done this work before. I was remembering.

I woke up the next morning with a vivid recollection of an intense dream I had during the night that had seemed so real, wondering what it had been about. I had no memory at that time of Marilyn "tapping" me, nor anything about "assignments" or "tasking a job."

There were people in a dark stormy sea, bodies bobbing on the surface along with debris like yesterday's thrown out trash. The number 37 kept popping onto my mind screen, and I had no idea what that meant. And then I turned on the TV and everything crashed into place as I watched the "breaking news" that morning.

The day before, Wednesday, November 24, 1999, a Chinese ferry carrying more than 300 people caught fire and capsized in rough seas off the northeast coast of China. Only 22 people survived. The 9,000-ton Dashun ferry, left the port at 1pm for what is normally a seven to eight-hour journey to the northeastern port of Dalian across the mouth of Bohai Bay.

It was forced to turn back because of extreme conditions as a fierce typhoon created huge waves that pounded and rocked the ferry. Some 20 miles out from port a fire was discovered on the lower vehicle deck, which was loaded with up to 60 cars. Distress signals were sent out at approximately 4:30pm.

The fire was apparently caused when one of the cars shifted and crashed into either another vehicle, an oil tank or the ferry's engines. By the time the crew reached the fire, it was out of control and hand-held fire extinguishers had no effect. Eventually the engines froze up, stranding the burning ferry in freezing winds and violent seas.

At approximately 11:50pm the ferry capsized and sank, equipment controlling the release of life preservers and lifeboats failed to work as the ferry started to go down. A tugboat was dispatched, trying for three hours to get close to the boat, but was unable to carry out a successful rescue because of the rough seas.

A horrific tragedy unfolded for those on board. In the dark of night, with nowhere to run or shelter from the smoke and fumes on board, many people decided to jump into the raging waters as the ferry began sinking. Around 20 to 30 people jumped ship to try and reach life buoys that the rescue vessel had thrown into the sea, but only one person was pulled to safety. Other passengers who were able to get into life rafts were swept into the freezing sea by the waves and drowned or died from exposure. One survivor swam in the violent sea for an hour, finally making it to shore. Another passenger survived by clinging to a life raft for four hours before being washed ashore. Another man said he smashed a cabin window when the ferry was sinking and then swam to the surface. He was rescued by a navy vessel that had arrived on the scene. Many corpses were found washed up along the shore, several dozen recovered from inside the shipwreck.

Who would I ever be able to tell about this? Who would ever believe me?

CHAPTER 7

The Sinking of the Kursk

Saturday, August 12, 2000

It was about 5:30 AM, about 30 minutes before I usually wake up to start the day. I felt the familiar "tapping" on my shoulder as I came to the surface and recognized Marilyn tapping me to get my attention and out of my dream state. There was a bit of an urgency to her insistent poking, and I asked her what was up. This wasn't the first time Marilyn has tapped me awake with a "job" to do, but this was different.

When I had "dreamed" of helping the undocumented, unticketed passengers on the Chinese ferry, I had just barely come to the surface of consciousness when Marilyn tapped me. I came up a bit to acknowledge the assignment and then dropped back to a deep but clear, lucid dream state. I was to do the release work for those unknown souls who would never be looked for as they were unregistered and on the boat with no paperwork. This was different. Somehow I knew that I was turning a sharp corner with this assignment, it would be uncomfortable for my 3Dness, and it was also important for my focus, discipline and growth for future service.

It had been a restless night for me, tossing and turning and feeling heavier and physically thicker, more sluggish than is normal for me. This would prove to be a portent of the importance of the mission I was being tasked with. Divine never "makes" me take these assignments.

Everything in life is always a choice. I had made the choice long ago to embrace and act on whatever gifts the universe offered me with trust and a strong sense of service. Regardless of how uncomfortable it may be for me in physical 3D, I trust Divine not to give me anything I cannot handle. I will answer the call as needed with gratitude, grace and focus on the task at hand.

Marilyn informed me that this mission would be different than the ferry incident last year. I had dropped back into sleep for that one, aware that something was going on during dreamtime, but not consciously aware of exactly what I was doing during that time. I awoke the next morning and saw the news of the ferry accident that I had been assigned to during the night. I had done the work while it was occurring in my time zone in real time, which was during the day in the Yellow Sea on the other side of the world.

For this mission, I will be freshly conscious from dream time. I was instructed to turn on the news, and I knew immediately what my assignment was. I just wasn't sure how or what I was to do. Marilyn told me, "You will know in good time." I didn't get upset with her this time for saying that. I simply waited until I knew without knowing when I was needed and what I was to do.

On Saturday, August 12, 2000, K-141 Kursk, an Oscar ll class nuclear-powered submarine of the Russian Navy suffered two explosions during a naval exercise in the Barents Sea, 160 miles from Norway. The 505 ft. long, 22,000-ton boat was now sitting at the bottom of the sea in over 350 feet of water. There are 118 souls on board. Spirit told me that this is all the information I was to have at this time and to "stand by."

I watched the brief breaking news piece, which had no other details of the event at this time; media speculation was going nuts with all kinds of scenarios. I turned off the TV and sat in the early summer morning, daylight beginning to blanket the quiet little village of Dilger. I dropped into the now familiar stillpoint of nothingness, resonating to the flow of expansive dimensionless awareness, and waited with no attachment to time, place or sense of self. The "call" would come soon enough. I had become accustomed to opening to Divine and letting go, to be "present" when the time came. I sensed that this was going to be a very powerful "exit-point" soul release experience not only for the souls I would serve but for myself as well. I had no idea how humbling it would be.

I drifted in and out of different layers of consciousness, dozing while seated straight up, drifting and rippling, in and out, up and down, like a gentle jellyfish aimlessly riding a calm sea. It was roughly 2 hours later when my mind screen came to life, and I was called to the sub lying dying at the bottom of the sea. I had not turned on the TV for any updates, so I had no knowledge of what was happening or being reported. I had only what Source was tasking me with; the energy, light, and compassion that was needed from me in the moment of NOW, and my desire and intent to be a conduit for healing, however that may be.

I noted the time on the clock. It was 7:34 AM in Dilger, 1:34 PM in the Barents Sea and the heart of a dying submarine. My awareness went directly to a compartment in the rear of the sunken sub where I noticed 23 men panicked but not terrified...yet. There was one young man who seemed to be in control of the group, commanding a calm presence and as much humor as possible under the circumstances. He must be an officer of some kind. He radiated hope to the others that help was on the way. Since I was here, I knew that this scene was going to shift soon.

The young officer had a piece of paper and was writing something in the dimly lit and cold compartment that already had water at around knee-level. I watched and rippled as much energy and light as I could to the entire compartment. I kept seeing the number 9 pop up on my mindscreen. I didn't question it or give it much attention, but simply let it brush its way across my mind like a wisp of hair on a puff of wind.

He finished writing whatever it was he was writing, and the conversation shifted back amongst the crew to possible escape through a hatch in the compartment. Hope was still strong that a rescue was coming, and there were too many unknowns about the viability of using the hatch. There was a problem of some kind with it. Perhaps stuck or damaged. This led to questions about what was on the other side of it if they did get it opened. They waited. So did I.

In a few minutes, one of the sailors seemed to go into distress of some kind. Heart attack. As he was going through the physical agony of the attack, grabbing his chest, he looked straight up at me where my light was hovering a few feet above and to his right. His face seemed to

38

soften a bit. I have no idea how he perceived my energy, but it seemed to ease his physical pain and panic. His eyes acknowledged that this was his exit-point, he accepted the grace of God, his physical heart stopped, and he slid down the bulkhead. The young officer who had been writing a while before, caught him before he slid into the water, which was now thigh-high, and with the help of two others, they draped his body across some kind of big pipe in the compartment.

The light was dimming, the air becoming thicker with oxygen running out, carbon monoxide gas filling the compartment, water rising ever so slowly. 9 9 9 9 running across my mindscreen. I let it move through as I focused my attention to the task at hand. One by one the men died, releasing their souls to Divine. There were others there like me who had their charges to tend to. I had three more of my releases left to go.

The young officer once again began to write. It was about 9:15 AM my time; 3:15 PM in the sub. As he put the note in his pocket, he looked directly up at me and got the sweetest smile of acceptance and appreciation on his face as he acknowledged my presence and why I was there. He nodded to me and then he mind-spoke to me. He never said what his name was but somehow was able to project onto my mindscreen an image of his beloved wife. This had never happened before. He said that this was his new bride of just a few months, the love of his life, and the image that he was taking with him when he exited 3D. I felt the strength of his love for this beautiful young woman. I almost physically felt how much he adored her, how he seemed to be ready to hold on to that passion, and let go of 3D into the Divine, back into the grace of God.

He said that all he ever wanted to be was a sailor. He was as devoted to and loved the Kursk as a man would love a mistress, he chuckled. His dedication to the Kursk was as powerful as his love for his lovely bride. He told me that they were the two greatest loves of his life. His new wife would grieve deeply for him. Yet, she knew that the love of the sea and his boat was just as important as she was, and she had loved him and accepted his mistress when she married him not so long ago. He was deep in the womb of his second love at the bottom of the sea. Whether this would give solace to his new wife, I had no idea. And it wasn't my concern. This vital soul was nearing his exitpoint and was very much at peace with it. As a conduit of energy and light, I simply optimized his vibration to make it as easy a soul release as possible, offering a higher frequency of light for him to ease his way to grace.

He held onto consciousness as long as possible as the precious little bit of air left in the compartment was being taken over by toxic carbon monoxide, the oxygen being sucked out. Conversation in the compartment had all but stopped as the remaining souls were so physically weak and tending to their own releases.

When this vibrant soul passed through his exitpoint, I looked at my clock, and it read 9:58 AM; 3:58 PM on the sub. Little did I know that this would not be the last I heard from this brave and lively spirit.

One of my other charges had also managed to scribble a note before becoming completely incapacitated. He gave me his name as Alex. I usually don't get names. And of course, I will never be able to prove any of this, so names don't matter. Somehow it was important for Alex to give me his name, perhaps giving back the "name tag" of 3D that had been given to him at birth. It gave him some freedom I suppose; to let it go. As he gave me his name, I sensed his physical pattern loosen, and with the note he had written, he quietly and without any struggle, softened his features, took his last breath, went unconscious, and slid into the now waist-high water. It was 11:41 AM my time; 5:41 on the Kursk.

The others like me were tending their charges in a similar fashion, the 23 souls slowly succumbing to the elements. The compartment was as peaceful and serene as a great cathedral. There was no struggle, no fear or panic or anger. Sweet surrender and release.

And then there was a blinding bright flash, and I got disoriented for a moment. An explosion of some kind? I brought my awareness back to where I had been present with my fourth and last charge of this assignment. He was gone. In the moment of the brilliant flash, he released his soul and had instantly exited. Assignment complete.

It was just after 12:00 noon my time. I was exhausted and hungry, and my four charges from the Kursk were free and at peace. I walked up to Betty's to integrate all that had just occurred.

I had a big lunch, didn't talk much to anyone, walked back to my little house, and with 9 9 9 9 wisping across my mindscreen as I sat on the sofa and closed my eyes, I slept the rest of the afternoon without so much as turning on the TV for any updates on the Kursk. I had my own version of the news "coverage" of the event.

Who would I ever be able to tell this to? Who would ever believe me?

CHAPTER 8

Confirmation

October 26, 2000

I was just beginning a four-day trip out of Pittsburgh. I had gotten to the airport, checked in for the trip, went down to the plane early to escape the masses of the flying public in the concourse and to have a bit of quiet time before the rest of the crew arrived.

I brought my bags onboard and took a seat in first class where I found an abandoned well-read copy of today's paper sitting conveniently on the seat next to me. Heaven only knows how many miles it had travelled or how many people had read it that day. It is a very good thing that I had already sat down; otherwise what I was reading would have buckled my knees and knocked me to the floor if I had been standing.

I don't recall the title of the article or who wrote it, or even what newspaper it was, except that this was the first of several articles from various media, as well as tv news reports, that came out over two months after the sinking of the Kursk. All I saw was "Kursk," and what had been discovered with the retrieval mission just a few days ago, after taking weeks to finally raise the sub.

Lt. Captain Dimitri Kolesnikov, 27, commander of the turbine room on the sub, was one of the first of four sailors whose bodies were retrieved since recovery operations began. Russian divers recovered his remains from the sub with a note stuffed in his pocket. Trapped over

300 hundred feet below the surface of the ocean in the doomed sub, the Captain scrawled a message beginning just after 1:00 pm, saying that 23 of them, out of a crew of 118, had been separated from the rest of the crew as a result of the explosions. The 23 had moved from compartments six, seven and eight into compartment nine, where there was still air and light.

At a candle-lighting ceremony today in Vidyayevo, the seaside village where most of the Kursk crew lived and raised families, the commander of the Russian Navy said the captain's message began legibly, as if written in a lighted room. But by the end it was nearly illegible, written "by feel." The note also indicated that two or three crewmen tried to escape the submarine through a specially built escape hatch in the ninth compartment where the survivors were gathered, and failed.

All efforts to find anyone alive was abondoned, and attention was focused on recovering the dead. But the ninth compartment might have remained dry for weeks, even up until rescuers would have been able to enter it.

The Kursk was participating in a naval exercise in the Barents Sea, off Russia's northwest coast, when an explosion thudded in its bow about 11:27 a.m. on Aug. 12. Two minutes and 15 seconds later a huge blast, registering a magnitude of 3.5, blew away the submarine's torpedo room and its command post, in the first and second compartments at the vessel's fore end. Various accounts say that the Kursk revved its turbines after the first blast; apparently trying to reach the surface, then plunged to the seabed after the second. Captain Kolesnikov had written his message between 1:34 p.m. and 3:15 p.m. that day. That suggested that at a minimum, he and 22 other crewmen survived at least four hours after the explosions. They had made it to compartment 9 where they were surviving on the remaining air in the compartment; waiting for rescue.

Captain Kolesnikov's message suggests that nearly everyone in the aft portion of the submarine initially survived the explosions, which devastated the two forward compartments that housed torpedoes and the submarine's command post. The Kursk's published crew roster states that 24 sailors were assigned to compartments six through nine, one more than the 23 cited in his note. What isn't clear is how long those 23 survived.

The captain's widow, Olga Kolesnikova, her face covered with tears, had said that her husband had a premonition of death before leaving on the Kursk's last voyage and left his dog tags, a crucifix and a poem as a remembrance.

The couple had married only this year. What was highlighted on TV and in the press were the Captain's last words:

"And when the time comes to die," he wrote in the poem, "though I chase such thoughts away, I want time to whisper one thing: My darling, I love you."

There are no words to describe the roller coaster ride of emotions and sensations that raced through me at reading this article. The soul release work I had done for the Kursk two months ago was being confirmed by the very crewmembers I had been tasked with to help "die." It was a mind-blowing shock on so many levels of my being. I was overwhelmed with stunned amazement, humility, and gratitude for my small part in the healing of a few of these souls, and dumbfounded at the gift I had received from beyond the grave by way of a lone discarded newspaper sitting in an empty first class seat. I don't believe in coincidences.

I completely fell apart and began sobbing like a baby, tears releasing all that was too big to hold inside. I don't cry easily, yet I cried from my deepest heart for the souls of that crew. I wept for the grace I had received and the honor I felt at being able to serve the crew with unique gifts not easily described or believed. I wept with gratitude for Divine's confirmation given to me via a newspaper article that gifted me with the validation that I indeed HAD done the work for these souls, and I had done it well. I cried until I had nothing left but amazement at the complex simplicity of life and the power of the human spirit. I felt calm joy, an immensely grateful heart, and an even greater desire to continue my path to serve as called upon, regardless of what people may say about it. As a result of this experience I felt more empowered with "detached compassion," "neutral awareness," and "divine indifference" that would prove to serve me well as life went on and the world changed.

Fortunately, I still had some time to collect myself before the rest of the crew showed up on the plane. I pulled myself together, clicked into flight attendant mode, splashed cool water on my face with little makeup adjustment, oh so grateful for waterproof mascara. Yes, the training wheels had definitely been blown completely off with this one. All I could do is wonder where this magnificent adventure called my life would lead me next? Yeah yeah. I can just hear Marilyn say, "You will know in time."

As the other crewmembers began trickling onto the plane and I was fully back in 3D, I wondered who I could possibly share this amazing and powerful soul-feeding experience with. Who would believe me? Best to keep this one to myself. For now.

Now, fast forward to 2002. I had just gotten to my hotel room on a layover in whatever city I was sleeping in that night. Flight attendants sleep around, all hotel rooms looking like the one from the night before. "Flight attendants sleep around." What a great bumper sticker.

My typical routine starts with a security check for boogie men in the bathroom, closet and under the bed. I look at the plaque on the inside of the door to see how many doorways I need to feel past to get to the closest set of stairs in case of a fire or earthquake. I then turn on the TV, kick off my shoes, get out the toiletries and put them in the bathroom before taking a shower and putting on my casual clothes.

On this particular evening, I made it as far as turning on the TV. I scrolled through the channels with the remote when my hand froze at a scene that almost knocked me over. I was stunned to see a young woman's face that somehow seemed familiar to me. I knew I had seen this beautiful and haunting face before, and it didn't take me long to recognize exactly who she was.

The hotel room occupant before me had apparently put the volume on mute, but there were subtitles at the bottom of the screen in English. I needed no volume to know that this was the beautiful young widow of Lt. Captain Dimitri Kolesnikov, commander of the turbine room of the Kursk, one of the souls I had been charged with after the tragic loss of the powerful sub. It was Dimitri's body with the note found in his pocket as they began to recover bodies from the depths of the watery tomb. It was the beautiful face of Olga that Dimitri had shown me before his passing, with the strength and power of his love for his bride of just four months before the Kursk tragedy. I knew her face because the love of her life had shown her to me before he died in compartment 9.

I turned up the volume, transfixed, as I watched the Discovery Channel documentary, "Raising the Kursk." I was still in uniform, sitting at the foot of the bed, mesmerized by the story of the fated sub, and footage of a video of Captain Kolesnikov excitedly showing his new bride, Olga, around his beloved Kursk. There was footage of the Captain, full of life and brimming with pride as he showed off the magnificent sub to Olga shortly before the ill-fated cruise that would separate them forever. I recognized him as soon as I saw his face on the screen and was moved to tears as I saw how alive he looked, so full of promise, hope, happiness. It was obvious how very much he loved his precious Olga, the beauty I was blessed to "see," as Dimitri released his soul and passed away. Olga would know how much she was loved from the recovered notes that I witnessed Dimitri writing in real time before his death in compartment 9 almost two years ago.

Dimitri projected a youthful confidence in himself, exuberance about life, and it was very apparent from the video that he was a fine officer who was proud of and loved his boat. In the interview with Olga, it was clear that she and Dimitri had been very much in love, looking forward to beginning a new life together. They were such a beautiful couple. She had admitted in the interview that she had been jealous of the Kursk as the other love in Dimitri's life.

I sat at the end of the bed watching the entire documentary, still in my uniform, not moving, mesmerized with by the entire story. My mind was all over the map trying to wrap itself around the jigsaw puzzle of human emotions I was experiencing at this moment. During commercial breaks, I closed my eyes and dropped into a state of gratitude and humility at receiving yet even more confirmation of the work I had done for the crew of the Kursk that I had been charged with on that August day in 2000.

It was beyond surreal to see Olga and Dimitri so human, normal, and so full of life, love and hope. On a human level it was heart-breaking to watch, yet my soul was full for being able to witness the human side of these two, feeling as if a circle had just been closed with this well-made documentary. I had a feeling that Dimitri was never far from Olga and that they would always have each other.

After the program was over, I took a shower, went to bed and fell into a very deep sleep. Just as I was moving into sleep from the edge of twilight consciousness, Dimitri's face moved onto my mind screen. He had the same peaceful, serene smile on his face that he had on his face as he looked directly at me before he died, allowing me to see the image of Olga as he released his soul to the higher dimension of light. I received a very poignant and heart-filled "thank you" from Dimitri through his gentle, playful and very expressive eyes. This was sweet closure for Dimitri and my role with the Kursk. Who would I ever be able to share this profound experience with? Who would ever believe me? And would it really matter if they believed it or not? Nope.

CHAPTER 9

The Day the World Stopped

I was clipping merrily along with life in the heart of the Allegheny Forest and the little hamlet of Dilger. I loved it here. Even though it is a huge contrast to the sun and the white sand beaches of Clearwater, Florida, pure nature is beautiful wherever you go. I was living in one of the most beautiful national forests in our country. Besides, as a flight attendant, if I want a warm sunny climate, I can fly to one almost any time I like.

I was content to hang out at Betty's, do some intuitive readings, my GatheringZ (spirit communication groups), a little ghost hunting for fun, and my occasional dreamtime "assignment" of soul release work. Most of my tasks were centered around transportation disasters. Tragic maritime, aviation, bus and train incidents around the world where there was a great loss of life seemed to have become my assigned area, my "charges" being many of those passengers and crew at the moment of soul release, their "exitpoint."

It had become quite natural for me to shift and drop into whatever frequency or vibration was being called for in order to do the work I do. The only way I can describe it is like a large round multi-ringed target with a black centered bull's-eye.

To me, the outer ring represents 3D human-hood The next ring in is the dimension or frequency that I tap into when I deal with the 3D energy of live people, animals, plants, inanimate objects, buildings and "things." Yes, this is quite possible and normal. Energy is just energy. It's how you observe it that counts.

Moving toward the center comes the ring of vibration that I shift to and engage when I am doing a "psychic" reading or healing session, whether in person or on the phone with someone. We have next a narrow sub-ring of this ring where the frequency is tweaked a bit for me to do CGI's (Computer Generated Insights) and automatic writing via the computer. Fun stuff. I've included a page on CGI's for you later in the book.

The next ring toward the center is the vibration of connecting with departed loved ones and pets that have passed into 4D. Finer, more multi-layered, more multi-dimensional. This is the heart-space of my GatheringZ, and my ability to "translate" the information from the departed into human. Even though the departed "live" mainly in the light and energy of 4D, I access several layers of dimensionality beyond 4D in order to receive easily more defined patterns of information. I can then pass on very clear details from the departed that I couldn't possibly have any knowledge of, easing pain, the sense of loss, giving closure, so that the living may go on living.

Moving toward the bull's eye, the dimensionality, the "feel," of the next ring becomes much more powerful, the entangled patterns of light and information vibrating beyond the speed of light. It is in this ring of multi-dimensionality that I am able to communicate clearly with those on life support, in a coma, nonresponsive or actively dying. I am bridging 3D into 4D with sprinklings of other dimensions that are interwoven for me to be fully present with these folks and wherever they "are" at the moment. This ring is more fluid and wave-like as the souls transition back and forth between dimensions, vibrational information being sent and received on many levels as they experience the journey out of 3D, into the light and energy of 4D.

Even though this ring is powerful, it is soft and easy for me, not as urgent or critical as the soul release work I do with a traumatic disaster that is happening in real-time. That ring is the core, the bull's eye of the target.

The black center spot on the target, the eye of the hurricane, the domain of my soul release work, is powerful beyond belief, and as you have already read, "soul release," "tasking an assignment," assisting my "charges" to die more easily, is not easy to explain. I hope I have painted decent enough word pictures for you to grasp at least a little of what I have attempted to convey. It isn't easy for me to put into human words that which is far beyond the realm of human comprehension.

The bull's eye on the target, the heart of the void, is a symphony of powerful multi-dimensional frequencies that I can only describe like a dog whistle at a pitch that no one can hear. The heart of the void vibrates so rapidly that it seems as if it is standing still, empty, nothing... stillpoint. This is the space of infinite potential, multiple dimensions of information, light and energy.

It is here in the bull's eye of infinite potential that I am able to assist souls to release in real-time as the disaster and trauma are happening around me. I am entangled in the nothingness of potential with no attachment to anything, yet fully aware, calm, compassionate, "present" in that moment to serve others as best I can.

I had gotten used to these different dimensional shifts and frequency changes, and knew which target "ring" would be most beneficial for the situation at hand. I had only gone to the bull's eye a few times in order to do my work as soul releaser. The sinking of the Kursk was the most physically taxing assignment for me to date. It was also the only task I had done so far while fully conscious and awake, helping my charges with their soul release in real-time as, over several hours, each accepted their exit-points and physically "died." It had taken a lot out of me physically, and it was the most rewarding exhaustion I had ever felt.

It had been a little over a year since the Kursk experience. Little did I know when I walked up to Betty's for coffee at 5:30 on this cool quiet forest morning, that the work I had done with the crew of the Kursk would be nothing compared to the assignment I would take on later this morning. It was Tuesday, September 11, 2001. The day the world stood still.

I had come back to my little house around 8:00 and turned the TV on to watch the early morning news, catching up on any newsworthy events I may have missed while sleeping. There didn't seem to be anything earth-shattering that had happened overnight. At about 8:46

on 9/11 that all changed, and as the day unfolded, the world changed forever.

As soon as I saw the first report of a "small plane" crashing into the North Tower of the World Trade Center at around 8:50, even in the confusion of the media trying to get updated information and the real story, I knew our country had just been attacked. I had been hearing "chatter" that summer while flying that I didn't want to believe. I immediately ran the short block back up to Betty's and urgently told them to turn on the TV, we were being attacked.

Everyone was glued to the screen watching it all unfold as more reports and speculation came in from the media. No one had mentioned terrorism...yet. Less than 10 minutes after I had gotten back to Betty's, at 9:03, we all witnessed the second plane hitting the South Tower, and there was no doubt about as to what was happening. We were under attack. The terror was just beginning.

The cafe got even more crowded as news of the attacks spread, everyone coming to Betty's, the heart of town, where people gathered to find out what is going on in the area. No one spoke. Everyone was stunned into silence as the news reports became less confusing and more accurate as to the true scope of what was going on.

At approximately 9:40, American Airlines flight 77 crashed into the Pentagon. At a little after 10:00, United flight 93 crashed into a field in Shanksville, PA. None of these jetliners were USairways planes, but that didn't matter. As a flight attendant, I couldn't even begin to imagine the terror of the flight crews as they realized that they were going to die and could do nothing to stop it or save their passengers or themselves. I felt the bone-deep terror of the crew as their planes were being flown erratically, pilots most likely already dead, and none of the people onboard knowing where or when the final impact would come.

I had to get home. As comforting as it was in the familiar surroundings, the safe normalcy of Betty's, I had to get home. I zombie-walked back to my house just in time to hear the news of flight 77 hitting the Pentagon. I sat mindlessly and shocked into stillness on the sofa, watching the breaking news with eyes that really didn't register anything but movement on the screen, deaf to any sound. My senses had shut down.

Somewhere around the sharp edges of my total numbness I felt a rippling wave of energy, a warm flow of consciousness moving near me. It was Marilyn, my deceased mother. Instead of her trademark "tapping" in order to get my attention, she presented herself more like just made and still warm cotton candy. Very sweet and gentle and radiating compassionate neutrality as she sat next to me on my sofa, I welcomed her company. Nothing was said for a moment as I felt my consciousness climbing out of the black hole of shocked numbness. My perception was becoming sharp and focused, calm and detached, as I realized that I had an important assignment to task. There were souls desperately in need of assistance...right now.

Marilyn looked at me with greater confidence in me than I felt as she got right to the point and said, "Your assignment is at the south side of the North Tower at the World Trade Center, where people are no longer thinking about WHETHER they are going to die, but HOW they are going to die. You and several others like you are tasked with releasing those choosing to jump."

I knew that this was an immediate real-time need and that I had to drop quickly and deeply into that bull's eye center of vibration of stillpoint, adjusting my energy pattern to the powerful frequency needed for this assignment. My task was to ease the soul release of those charged to my care as best I could. I took a deep breath, dropped my awareness with a prayer asking for the grace of Divine that I serve with as much light as I could in order to task this assignment for the peaceful soul release of all my charges. I had no idea how many souls I would be tasked with assisting, and it didn't matter. I am on this planet for service to others, and this is the greatest service I can imagine.

I found myself hovering about mid-way between the south side of the North Tower and the South Tower, which had been hit many floors lower than the first tower. It became apparent that I was tasked with jumpers from floors 87 and 88 on that side of the North Tower. The smoke was rolling out of the building, debris was flying everywhere, the heat like a blast furnace, yet I and others like me on assignment with me, were clearly seen by the people teetering in window frames, deciding how to die. I looked around, and each of us servers seemed as if we were all enclosed in some sort of personal, transparent, protective bubble that shimmered an otherworldly, faint silvery-turquoise radiance.

The atmosphere in the bubble was comfortable. I felt weightless, I was breathing pure, clean air, the temperature was pleasant, a sharp sense of awareness filling every atom of my body as I waited for my first charge at their exitpoint moment. The irony of the comfort I was feeling in the bubble versus the absolute horror and chaos that the people in the building were feeling didn't go unnoticed. I had no emotions or feelings attached to that. I simply took it all in, motivated even more by spirit to serve these souls as best I can.

There were others like me in their bubbles who had been tasked not with the jumpers, but with the souls who were so confused and panicked, gasping for air and blinded by smoke, that they didn't realize they were at the window's edge, and either fell out or were pushed out by other equally crazed souls desperate to get a breath of air.

My assignment was the jumpers from the 87th and the 88th floors on the south side of the North Tower. These floors were below the point of impact of the jetliner that hit between floors 94 and 98 on the northeast side of the tower. The intense heat was already buckling floors beneath the impact point. There were toxic fumes, billowing black smoke, and random fires that set combustible materials on fire, creating a toxic blast furnace inferno of impossible escape. So many people in living hell.

The jumpers seemed to come from everywhere in a steady stream, more from the other sides of the tower than mine, but still, these souls were falling like raindrops. I held my neutral detachment in order to offer all the light I could for the 9 souls whose release I was tasked with. This was the toughest assignment of my life, and I had to hold steady for my charges. It was not easy, but I held the course until, with one last look in my direction, seeing me however it was appropriate for them to perceive me in that moment, one by one they accepted their exitpoint. When it was their time, they each got that sweet sense of calm surrender on their faces, peace seemed to ripple through them, they let go of their grip on the dying building, and let go.

Even though it would take several seconds for their bodies to reach the ground, as soon as they chose to let go, their souls were already releasing. The jumpers felt no sensation of falling. There was no more fear or panic or confusion. They let go of that when they chose to jump. As soon as they chose, they were free.

I witnessed a magnificent pattern of shimmering radiance unique to each soul rising out of each of their bodies as they let go. I have no words to describe the infinite brilliant colors of God. I'm not going to try. Even attempting to describe it in our limited language of 3D would tarnish the very essence of Divine and the pure beauty of grace.

It had taken only a couple of minutes to task my assignment and release my 9 beautiful charges to the light, but I was exhausted. I gently brought my awareness back to 3D, my sofa and the TV with the continuous coverage of the terrorist attacks that had just stopped the world. Marilyn had shown up just after flight 77 had hit the Pentagon at around 9:40 a.m. I now looked at the clock and saw that it was 9:52. Only 12 minutes to task my assignment and be "present" for my charges. I was physically spent, sapped of all energy, and felt an incredible sense of gratitude, joy and peace, so very blessed to be who I am. I sat silently on my sofa, no Marilyn around, recalibrating myself back to 3d and the reality of what was going on.

Seven minutes later the South Tower collapsed. Approximately eight minutes after that flight 93 was flown into the ground in a field near Shanksville, PA. The passengers had regained control of the plane, and knowing they were going to perish in a terrorist plot to use the jetliner as a bomb to hit somewhere in DC, probably aiming for the White House, they bravely crashed it before it could reach its target. Approximately twenty minutes after flight 93 dove into the ground, the North Tower collapsed.

So very tired now, I laid down, numbing my senses to what was going on. I allowed the steady drone of voices on TV to help me drop into a deep dreamless sleep for seven hours. Waking a bit cobwebby but fairly alert, I sat up. Marilyn was sitting at the other end of the sofa.

"Hey sleepy head," she said with softness in her voice.

"Hey. Tough day," I replied, banishing the cobwebs and waking up completely.

"You did well with your assignment today, Keli. You held the light powerfully for the easy soul release of your charges. I know how difficult it was for you to stay on task and not to get emotional or attached to the trauma. That took a lot of your energy, but you held strong. Good job." And then Marilyn was gone.

I have no recollection of what I did the rest of that evening or the next day. I do remember I got emails and phone calls from everyone I knew to see where I was and if I was okay. I don't remember if I talked to anyone or not. What I do remember at the core of my soul is that I served 9 souls in a unique way with a lot of love and light that day. And that's enough to feed my soul for a very long time.

And I never told anyone about the "work" I had done with my 9 jumpers from the south side of the North Tower that day. Until now. Now you know. And how do you believe something as incredible as the story I have just told you? I have no idea. Doesn't matter.

In case you are not familiar with the timeline of that fateful day, here is a compilation from various news sources of the chain of events that took place on 9/11:

8:00 a.m. - American Airlines Flight 11, Boeing 767 with 92 people aboard, takes off from Boston's Logan International Airport for Los Angeles.

8:14 a.m. - United Airlines Flight 175, Boeing 767 with 65 people aboard, takes off from Boston's Logan airport for Los Angeles.

8:21 a.m. - American Airlines Flight 77, Boeing 757 with 64 people aboard, takes off from Washington Dulles International Airport for Los Angeles.

8:40 a.m. - Federal Aviation Administration notifies North American Aerospace Defense Command's Northeast Air Defense Sector about suspected hijacking of American Flight 11.

8:41 a.m. - United Airlines Flight 93, Boeing 757 with 44 people aboard, takes off from Newark International Airport for San Francisco.

8:43 a.m. - FAA notifies NORAD's Northeast Air Defense Sector about suspected hijacking of United Flight 175.

8:46 a.m. - American Flight 11 crashes into the north tower of the World Trade Center.

9:03 a.m. - United Flight 175 crashes into the south tower of the World Trade Center.

9:08 a.m. - FAA bans all takeoffs nationwide for flights going to or through airspace around New York City.

9:21 a.m. - All bridges and tunnels into Manhattan closed.

9:24 a.m. - FAA notifies NORAD's Northeast Air Defense Sector about suspected hijacking of American Flight 77.

9:26 a.m. - FAA bans takeoffs of all civilian aircraft.

9:31 a.m. - President Bush, in Florida, calls crashes an "apparent terrorist attack on our country."

9:40 a.m. (approx.) - American Flight 77 crashes into Pentagon.

9:45 a.m. - FAA orders all aircraft to land at nearest airport as soon as practical. More than 4,500 aircraft in the air at the time.

9:48 a.m. - U.S. Capitol and White House's West Wing evacuated.

9:59 a.m. - South tower of trade center collapses.

10:07 a.m. (approx.) - United Flight 93 crashes in Pennsylvania field.

10:28 a.m. - North tower of World Trade Center collapses.

11:00 a.m. - New York Mayor Rudolph Giuliani orders evacuation of lower Manhattan.

12 p.m. - Amtrak, Virginia Railway Express, and MARC shut down rail service.

1:04 p.m. - From Barksdale Air Force base in Louisiana, Bush announces U.S. military on high alert worldwide.

2:51 p.m. - Navy dispatches missile destroyers to New York, Washington.

3:07 p.m. - Bush arrives at U.S. Strategic Command at Offutt Air Force Base in Nebraska.

4 p.m. - Northbound lanes of Interstate 395 reopen.

5:25 p.m. - Empty 47-story Seven World Trade Center collapses.

6 p.m. - Trade Center Building No. 7, another building in the complex, collapses.

6:30 p.m. - About 150 lawmakers gathered on the Capitol's steps. Some — including House Speaker Dennis Hastert (R-Ill.) — give speeches, then the group observes a moment of silence, followed by a spontaneous chorus of "God Bless America." George Washington Memorial Parkway reopens.

6:58 p.m. - President Bush returns to the White House after stops at military bases in Louisiana and Nebraska.

7:30 p.m. - Defense Secretary Donald Rumsfeld announces that the Pentagon will open for business on Wed., Sept. 12.

8:30 p.m. - President Bush addresses the nation again, summing up the attacks as "evil, despicable acts of terror" and quoting from the Psalm 23: "Even though I walk through the valley of the shadow of death, I fear no evil for you are with me."

I read several months later that they estimated that there had been about 200 jumpers (or fallers) from both the North Tower and the South Tower, with no way to identify anyone. There were just no remains in the heaps of rubble that would have helped, leaving many people still listed as missing.

There were also reports about the North Tower jumpers from witnesses that survived the collapse of the South Tower, the tower that collapsed first. They reported that they had been told by building management that they were safe and to stay inside where they would be protected from debris from the North Tower. When they saw all the bodies falling like rain from the North Tower, a mere 120 feet away, they were motivated to get out of the South Tower. Hundreds of people evacuated from the building, and an estimated 1400 lives were saved as a result. The dying saved the living.

On the first anniversary after 9/11, a memorial service was held in Dilger. Among others who represented the fallen firefighters and law enforcement officers that day, I was asked to represent all of the flight crew members who perished, receiving an American flag in their honor. I wore my flight attendant uniform, stomach in knots, struggling with emotions as I humbly accepted the flag for the flight attendants and pilots who died. I worked hard to not completely break down, tears stinging my eyes, and was so very grateful that I didn't have to say anything but "thank you." It was a tough day. It was a rewarding day. I was honored and grateful to have been included.

I bought a wooden flag display case and plaque for the flag and then took it up to Betty's where I asked that it be displayed. The flag wasn't mine. The town had held the memorial service to remember all of those who perished that day, and Betty's Cafe, the heart of Dilger, was where the flag belonged. I told Carol that if anything ever happened to the cafe, to display the flag in the post office. After Carol passed a few years ago, I was contacted and asked what I would like done with the flag. I told them that it is the town's flag, not mine, and to please take it over to the post office to be put on display. I got word that the flag is indeed now on display in the Dilger post office.

CHAPTER 10

Valentine's Day 2009
"Jack"

I never question any trips I get because something always occurs to let me know why I got the trip, why I'm flying with the people I'm flying with, and why I get the passengers I get. This little one-day trip I picked up proved the true perfection of what I like to call "divine dance."

I picked up the out-and-back trip down to Punta Cana, in the Dominican Republic. One flight down there, put my face in the sun for a few minutes, and then one flight back to Charlotte. I took the senior position ("A") on the trip, and we were on an Airbus 319. Two flight attendants sit on the front jumpseat for take-off and landing. The "C" flight attendant who sat next to me is a very upbeat, attractive, outgoing, personable, warm, and as I found out on the flight down to Punta Cana, a very special man. He gave me permission to use his story, asked me to use it, as long as didn't use his his name in the book, so I will just call him "Jack."

I had not flown with Jack before, even though I had seen him around the system in past years. While we were in the front galley getting ready to receive passengers, somehow it came out in our chatting that he had a daughter who died a few years ago from cancer. She was six when she died.

I can't remember how this conversation got started, however, as soon as he said that he had a child who had died, her beautiful face and spunky personality popped up on my psychic screen. I told him that she is fine, still feisty, and a gorgeous, healthy little girl. He didn't ask me how I knew. He wasn't shocked at all. He simply agreed with me that she is all of that and more, he knows she's fine, and he knows that he will see her again in time.

We talked a lot on the jumpseat about religion, faith, my work, and most especially about his family's experience with hospice, and how much they helped them with the passing of his precious jewel with the beautiful blue eyes. He was an amazing breath of fresh air with his attitude about life, death and what great support hospice had been. His was a truly a remarkable story from the heart of a man who has experienced not only the loss of a child, but had the assistance, compassion and the supporting heart of hospice to help his daughter and his family through that terrible time.

I knew with absolute certainty from flying with Jack that I wanted to see how I could work with hospice using my psychic gifts, soul release "assignments," and mediumship, to ease the pain of the living as well as the dying. To be "present with the presence of death" via the portal of hospice, resonated very strongly with me.

Flying with Jack, hearing his story, was bringing me to hospice in order to use my gifts for an even greater purpose, and to take me to deeper dimensions of myself.

As soon as I got home, I registered for the next volunteer training class, which would be in a couple of weeks. I went in for my one-on-one interview with Sallie, the head of volunteer services, and told her that I would like to work with hospital hospice patients instead of doing home visits. She found this interesting as they had only one other volunteer doing hospital visits. Apparently hospital visits, especially with the actively dying and their families were harder emotionally on the volunteers, and the majority prefer home visits. She wanted me to be very clear that hospital visits can be pretty tough, and that you never know exactly what you may be walking into with the patient, their condition or the family dynamic.

Feeling as if I had to be completely honest and open, I told Sallie about my gifts, what I do with them, and how I feel that hospice and I would be a good fit. She listened intently, smiled and said, "I am so glad you have come to us. You are exactly what we pray for."

She scheduled me for my mandatory TB test, invited me to the next volunteer class, and gave me a huge bear hug before I left her office with a heartfelt, "I can't thank you enough, Keli. I am so grateful you came in." Was she kidding? I was the one who was grateful to be there. Little did I know how just how powerful working with hospice patients was going to change my life. It wouldn't be long before I found out. The most amazing hospice experience I have had to date was to be my first patient...and my greatest experience with Divine grace.

CHAPTER 11

Hospice

The term "hospice" can be traced back to medieval times when it referred to a place of shelter and rest for weary or ill travelers on a long journey. This was the name applied to specialized care for dying patients in 1967.

Hospice has brought awareness to the importance of patients as individual, unique human beings deserving of individual needs and rights, exploring ways to improve the process of dying and shed light on the needs of patients during this important passage of life.

In 1974, the first hospice in the U.S., the Connecticut Hospice opened. As more people learn what hospice offers, they choose hospice care for their loved ones or themselves.

Dying veterans represent a large percentage of all deaths in the U.S. The number of Veterans needing care is growing. These men and women, several thousand a month, are dying in the homes and communities in which they live. Many die alone.

Honoring our nation's Veterans includes supporting them with dignity and respect throughout their lives, even at life's end when it may not be as easily done.

CHAPTER 12

NODA and Death DOULAS

NODA (No One Dies Alone)

(No One Dies Alone) was founded in November 2002 by Sandra Clark, CCRN, at Sacred Heart Medical Center in Eugene, Oregon. She was doing her rounds on a rainy night

No One Dies Alone (NODA) is a program where volunteers keep watch over those who are dying. When hospital patients who have no one to visit them are in the process of passing away, the volunteers keep vigil at their bedsides by holding their hand, talking to them, or just being present to ensure they won't be alone in their final moments. The NODA program has won several awards and has inspired hospitals around the U.S. and beyond to create similar programs.

Patients in need are identified by their health care team when death is expected within a few days and typically when no family or friends are nearby. A NODA vigil is then activated to provide a reassuring presence at the bedside of the dying patient for as long as needed.

Death Doulas

A Death Doula is a non-medical person trained to care for someone holistically (physically, emotionally and spiritually) at the end of life. Death Doulas are also known around the world as: end of life coaches, soul midwives, transition guides. death coaches, doula to the dying, end of life doulas, death midwives, and end of life guides.

Death Doulas are people who support people in the end of life process, much like a midwife or doula with the birthing process. It is a new non-medical profession that recognizes death as a natural, accepted, and honored part of life. One might say that death midwifery is to hospice palliative care as birth midwifery is to obstetrics.

CHAPTER 13

Baby "X"

I rocked rhythmically back and forth in the rocking chair as I held the fragile, tiny four-day-old bundle like a small cocoon in my arms, drinking in the calm, gentle silence of the room. I looked down at this beautiful sleeping infant, appearing so warm and comfortable with his tiny-fisted hands tucked into his chest, up under his chin, wrapped tightly in his little blanket. Snuggly encased like a papoose, with the perfect face of an angel, with luscious soft, dark curly hair, this little guy radiated an energy I can only describe as pure puppy contentment. Perhaps what an abandoned stray puppy feels like after someone has rescued him from a cold, desolate dark night, bringing him home, cleaning him up, giving him some warm milk, wrapping him up in a clean dry towel and just holding him close, keeping him safe. There is no real defined emotion; just a sort of detached gratitude for its survival, simple, comfortable contentment and just "being." I drank in the puppy contentment from this sweet spirit of a newborn, humbled to be able to experience him without any interruption.

At that moment, the world stopped. Time, distance and space didn't exist. And I knew without knowing that I was exactly where I was supposed to be at that moment. I was somewhere between time and space, if that makes any sense. I was somewhere between thoughts, even though I had an awareness that thoughts were yapping out there somewhere, and I just didn't care. I was somewhere between emotions even though I was aware they were floating around like gossamer threads somewhere. I was completely detached. My senses were more acute than ever even though I felt a strange sense of neutrality. I could even hear the normally silent second hand on the clock up on the wall ticking away time that didn't exist. It sounded like a soft measured heartbeat that allowed me to spiral deeper into this sweet cotton candy moment, detaching from the world of 3D humanness even more.

I was right there, right now, my senses heightened, and nothing mattered but "now." What I was feeling was an indescribable fluid and expansive state of bliss. It isn't a place. It isn't tangible. Yet it is as real as reality itself. There is no possible description of it or explanation for it. Bliss just is. Some dimension I seemed to have accessed by not being attached to anything, not even the moment. The physicality around me, was a ripple, "thinking" not even an option. And I was content not to care about 3D at the moment.

Spiraling like a feather down a dark yet wondrous wormhole of some kind, I felt everything, yet was attached to nothing at the same time. I felt so humbled and so blessed to be here it made my heart almost ache.

As I gazed down at the face of this beautiful sleeping angel of perfection in my arms, and this remarkable sensation that filled every molecule of my being, it was difficult for me to wrap my mind around the fact that this baby was dying and probably wouldn't live more than a couple of more days. Baby X was born four days ago with a genetic complication that wouldn't allow most of his organs to form or function correctly, especially his liver and kidneys. The parents were told he had no chance of "thriving" and he wouldn't live more than a few days, if that. The family couldn't have him at home to be there to take care of him around the clock. They were young and both new to the military, just starting out, and the baby needed specialized care that they couldn't offer.

Baby X was at the hospital where he could be treated, cared for, made as comfortable as possible, given human touch and attention that would ease his passing. Hospice was administering just enough medication to keep his pain level down the tiny babe was touched and held as much as the nurses and volunteers could do it. There were several nurses who couldn't even hold Baby X. It was too painful for them to bond with this little guy knowing he would die within a matter of days, if not hours. I suppose most of them were mothers and saw the faces of their own children in that tiny bundle. Baby X was given small amounts of liquid nourishment through a tube taped to his tiny head, running through one of his nostrils and into his stomach. I guess he needed some energy in order to leave his body comfortably, and they didn't want him to get upset or cry because of being hungry. The crying would have traumatized his little body, making his passing even harder on him as well as his family and caregivers.

I sat and rocked Baby X quietly for what seemed liked minutes, but in real time (and I use that word loosely) was almost exactly three hours. They were the most incredible and poignant three hours of my life to this point.

I drifted down into the gentle silence of a timeless wormhole with this little bundle, this tiny, powerful divine spirit, and he took me on an adventure that defies all explanation. As we deliciously spiraled into the depths, I knew I was on an adventure that would feed my soul and open my heart wider than I had ever known. In that three-hour visit, Baby X would take me into the core of all that is, into the heart of Divine, into a perfect state of grace.

There was activity in the hospital hallway, but it seemed as if Baby X and I had the world to ourselves. As I rocked with the baby and got into a hypnotic rhythm forward and back, forward and back, I looked down at his sweet, peaceful, trusting face, reflecting the perfection of God. He was swaddled snugly in his little blue blanket and appeared to be comfortable. As I held him in the crook of my right arm, I slipped my left baby finger into the palm of one of his little crossed fists, feeling that I did it more for my comfort than his.

Interesting. Looking down into this precious perfect face, skin as soft as velvet, it was hard to wrap my brain around the fact that this angel wasn't supposed to have survived this long, and he was going to die very soon. Then the strangeness started rippling in. The air seemed "charged" with some kind of energy, an altered sense of time and space penetrating the space. Like the way the air changes before a powerful thunderstorm, there was a definitive shift in the pressure of the room. This felt a bit different from my previous experiences with the soul release "assignments" I have been tasked to do. Different than the ferries in China, different than the experiences with the crew of the Kursk.

Maybe it had to do with this baby, so brand new to 3D, and his brief existence in this world. Perhaps it had to do with my calling to be a hospice volunteer, and the pattern of the heart of hospice was entangled with my gift of assisting with soul release. This was just a different type of "sensing" for me. All I know is that I was on heightened awareness. And I was paying attention big time.

Almost like a movie somehow superimposed over this perfect face, all of the sudden I got the sense of a scene of a tall hill in the fall, a giant oak tree at the top of the hill, thick trunk, and strong branches. The leaves were falling from the tree like popsicle-colored feathers caught on a breeze. There were bright orange, brilliant yellow, rich crimson leaves swirling off the branches, finding their way to a huge pile surrounding the base of the tree in a riot of color. Out of this mound of leaves came an intoxicating, contagious child-like laughter. Something was moving beneath the surface of the leaves. There was more than one "something" rummaging under there.

Suddenly, a medium-sized short-haired black dog came rushing out, pink tongue hanging out of the side of its mouth, long tail curved up and wagging furiously, loping out of the leaves, around the back side of the tree and out of sight. I seemed to be some silent observer in this movie, standing about fifteen feet to the left side of the tree, unseen by the romping dog. The delicious laughter continued as did the movement in the leaves. And then, breaking out of the pile of popsicle-colored leaves, a beautiful vibrant little boy, about six years old, light brown hair, innocent shoe-button brown eyes, and a splash of freckles across his little pixie nose, burst out of the pile, huge grin on his face.

I could feel the briskness of the autumn breeze, invigorating and energetic, signaling the coming natural dormancy, stillness, and starkness of winter. I heard the crispness of those wildly colorful leaves, noticing that even though it was obviously autumn, the grass on the hill beneath the stark oak gracefully shedding its leaves was a rich, almost emerald green. The grass was thick, long, and perfectly manicured. The sharp contrast between the woodsy smell of the oak, its dying leaves and the faint summer-fresh fragrance of the soft green grass, created an intoxicating "scentual" dance of nature. I was being drawn into this amazing movie through all of my senses. It was too incredible and mesmerizing to resist.

The magnificent little boy broke out of the leaf pile laughing and giggling, flinging his arms and tossing leaves up in the air, many of them sticking in his hair, some caught in the weave of his navy blue cable-knit sweater. He ran after the dog behind the tree as if they were playing a game of tag with each other, and he was "it." The dog began barking playfully, and the little boy began laughing even harder. I felt the chilly breeze on my face at the same time I felt the warmth of the sun shining through the near-naked branches in a bright cloudless sky. I could hear the wind blowing the dying crackling leaves off the branches of the majestic oak.

I could see everything in such vivid color it was surreal; this riot of flying leaves like butterflies against a brilliant blue sky. I could smell the intoxicating mixture of the woodsy leaves and the soft green grass. I could almost taste the richness of this moment like a blend of sweet otherworldly nectars. As I observed this incredible little movie, astounded at how heightened my physical senses had become, I noticed the little freckled-face and rumpled leafy hair peeking around the large oak, looking directly at me. It was unsettling for a brief moment that this little one could see me, wherever I was. Then, with all my physical as well as psychic senses in high gear, I felt a need to just "play." I wanted more than anything to be right here right now and as present as I could be at the moment.

The tiny infant in my arms was somehow magically taking me down a most remarkable rabbit hole. The little boy peered around the tree trunk, and I psychically said, "I see you little man."

The instant I said those words in my mind, Baby X, the dying infant that had no response to any stimulation at all, weakly squeezed my finger wrapped in his tiny fist. I didn't imagine it. I didn't make it up. The baby squeezed my finger as if he was acknowledging this movie playing out and was enjoying it as much as I. He knew what was going on. What in the world was happening here? I dropped even deeper into the ripples of this magical experience with a squeeze of the tiny hand, enthralled with where it was taking me.

The little boy in the movie seemed very surprised that I could see him and hid back behind the tree again. In less than a minute, he peeked his little head back around the tree, this time with a big grin on his face. The black dog came scampering out barking, seeming willing both of us to play some more.

Somewhere over the rise of the hill, a big red kite with a long tail came sailing into view. With the background of azure blue sky, it looked like it had been painted into the scene. The kite was a brilliant red, had a long knotted cloth tail, and it stubbornly gave the wind a run for its money, as if defying nature itself. The boy and I saw the kite at about the same time, and looking at each other, we both took off running after it, barking black dog frolicking after us. Somehow, I had just gone from being an observer to becoming part of the movie, and I was loving it.

We played, romped, laughed and threw leaves high in the sky as if tossing a giant salad. We were seeing who could toss the most the highest, catching just the right breeze that would carry the colorful leaves wherever they were going to fly; lovely butterflies following their destiny without a care. The black dog jumped up and bit at as many as he could, barking joyously, joining us in this purely innocent, wonderfully simple and wordless moment of bliss where time didn't exist. We played, laughed, and giggled with an expansive understanding that was beyond anything human.

After a time, I knew without knowing that it was time to come back out of this incredible movie, and as I looked into the perfect face of Baby X, I psychically thanked him for the wondrous time we had just shared. Then he smiled. Eyes closed, peaceful little face, no ability to show expression or react to external stimuli, Baby X smiled the purest angelic smile I have ever felt. I was moved to tears at an experience that I would never be able to explain to anyone. Who would believe me?

Completely back in the room now, aware of the surroundings, I looked up at the ticking clock and realized what had seemed like mere minutes of time had actually been three hours. Who was this magnificent impish little boy running in the leaves, chasing bright red kites in the autumn wind with his playful black dog? What did he have to do with Baby X, the dying newborn?

Maybe a past life or future incarnation of the soul of Baby X? Who knows? All I knew with absolute certainty was this had been one of the most remarkable three hours of my life. Baby X would be one of the most memorable souls I would ever encounter.

Sweet Baby X, born only five days ago with the cards stacked against him, died quietly and easily the next day in the arms of his mother.

I was a brand new, inexperienced hospice volunteer. Baby X was my first patient. He was my first teacher and guide for upcoming indescribable journeys of grace with hospice patients at the edge of life. Beyond space and time, beyond anything human and 3D, my humbling and amazing experiences with hospice were just beginning. Baby X had set the bar of true perfection and divine grace.

CHAPTER 14

2010—Miss Lucie

I had been working for the past seven days in my living sitcom of the airline industry, coping the best I was able with increasingly ungrateful and demanding passengers. I was ready for the wonderful contrast of hospital visits with the dying and their families. Sounds a bit twisted, yes? But you have been able to peek through my eyes a tiny bit and get a little glimpse of how wonderful and humbling hospice volunteering is to me. It's nice to be appreciated. I have yet to have one patient say anything negative about hospice. Everyone is so very grateful to have had the services of hospice to make the ordeal of death as easy for the family as well as for the patient.

When I took my volunteer training, we went around the room introducing ourselves, saying why we were there. Typically, people become volunteers because they have had a good experience with hospice caring for a dying loved one. They were able to see what a wonderful organization it is and want to offer that same service and comfort to others. I was panicking a little as my turn was coming up to explain why I was there. I had no experience with hospice, hadn't had anyone close to me die. My mother, Marilyn's death, had been pretty quick, we hadn't had hospice, and I couldn't very well tell everyone about the great relationship I now had with my dead mother. Somehow I don't think that would go over very well. There is no easy way to explain that I simply wished to offer my gifts and unique abilities to communicate with people, regardless of their state of consciousness. When the introductions got to me, and I introduced myself, saying I was there because that's where I was supposed to be right now. And here I am.

I called the office this July morning, and Sallie told me that we had one patient at the hospital to visit. Lucie, ninety-seven, a nursing home patient they had admitted yesterday, had dementia and confusion and was mostly nonresponsive. Sallie told me Lucie seemed to get very upset and agitated when family or friends came into the room, so the room was kept quiet and darkened, and there were few visitors now that she was becoming more nonresponsive and inactive. The extreme agitation and excitability is typical for some dying patients as they get closer to death. Ninety-seven years old. I was looking forward to meeting Lucie and hoped that she would share with me how life had been for her. What a history and what stories she must have.

When I got to the hospital, I asked at the nursing station if it would be okay for me to go in and see her. Since I was with hospice, they felt it would be fine, she probably wouldn't get excited or upset. I quietly pushed open the half-closed door, and in the semi-darkness lay a fragile little black woman, seemingly asleep, breathing shallowly but appeared to be comfortable and without oxygen. I walked over to the side of the bed and softly called her name. She opened the richest, deepest chocolate brown eyes I had ever seen, trying to focus on the voice she was hearing through the gossamer cloud of her confusion. She targeted my eyes with her own deep brown, and it was as if this frail little sparrow had a bright, otherworldly wisdom shining out from of the windows of her soul. There was a profound sharp attention beyond what was happening to her dying body. Looking into those chocolate pools of decades of experience, I knew without knowing that she had lived well and was dying just as well. She didn't communicate with me the way Josh had done. There wasn't any charge to the air or sharpening shifting of the senses. There was simply an understood voice with no words, and through her eyes she was speaking volumes. She was delirious, and even though she was making an effort to speak, she just wasn't able to. Nor did she didn't need to.

Her eyes held mine as I introduced myself and I thought-asked her if there was anything I could do to make her more comfortable. She had a sweet, gentle spirit, and through those shoe button eyes she conveyed she had lived a good life, and she was ready to have Jesus carry her home to be with God. She said she got agitated when her family came in because they couldn't handle her death, which meant they couldn't handle their own mortality.

Everyone dies in their own way, in their own limited time, according to their individual personality. This is why so many people release their souls when a loved one who has been sitting with them for hours or even days, steps out to go to the restroom or get a cup of coffee. If you are with someone when they die, you are with them because they want you there. If you wanted to be there and couldn't get there in time, take this as a loving gesture of the dying person to spare you from your own humanness.

Miss Lucie said, "I am a very private person who wants to die alone in the comfort and light of my Savior Jesus rather than to be miserable in a room full of pain and fear from my family that don't understand that you ain't got to be afraid of dying and going home to God."

Her eyes seemed to get a distant and longing look in them as she continued, "That's why I figure death gonna come in the middle of the night when the world quiet and most peaceful, and I can truly embrace the glory of going home." She looked like an angel.

I only stayed a few minutes with Miss Lucie. Lucie would die with the strength of her faith as powerfully as she had lived it. I leaned over and brushed a piece of her coarse wild gray hair back off her forehead, and she reached for my hand as I was bringing my arm back down. She gave me a weak squeeze with her thin, knobby fingers, looked into my eyes as if she were looking into my heart, and I heard her gentle soul thanking me for visiting. She told me I was a good girl and to have a blessed life. I returned the blessing with a smile and a prayer, pulled the covers up a little more snuggly, and left Miss Lucie to enjoy her journey.

Dying is different for everyone. My experience with each dying patient is as unique as each soul, and I am always humbled and grateful to be a part of this phase of their life. There seems to be a certain intimacy between each patient and me; something intangibly sacred that is so very special, private and ironically, full of vitality and light. Many hospice nurses, social workers, doctors, and clergy, can relate to this phenomenon. Even though they have to serve and care for them with a certain sense of clinical detachment, I'm sure each one of them has their own special intimacy with their dying patients they rarely share with anyone else. I have heard a few heart-warming stories from medical caregivers of the passing of patients...how they sensed or "felt" something remarkable, light and loving as they took their last breath.

By the time these souls are admitted to the hospital for me to visit, they are in their eleventh hour, and I generally don't have much time with them. The other caregivers, hospital personnel and hospice staff have gotten to know the patient and their families over time, been with them through the entire illness, getting close to them, and now are here for the final goodbye. That has to be tough, and I so admire all caregivers for what they do to ease life before death.

Miss Lucie did indeed release her soul that sultry July night at around 3:45 AM. I was sound asleep at home when she "visited" me in my dream-time that night. Chocolate brown eyes, as soft and sweet as I had seen them earlier that morning when I had visited her in the hospital, now filled full of an otherworldly light that I can only describe as absolute bliss and pure grace. She smiled at me with a beautiful childlike innocence and purity, mind-thoughted to me, "The glory of God is real. Glory be to God," and then she was gone. It was a quick flash of a visit. I guess Miss Lucie just wanted me to know that she had truly made it home. When I called Sallie the next morning to check on patients, I asked specifically about Miss Lucie. She said that she had died in the night. I asked Sallie if they had a time of death. 3:47 AM.

CHAPTER 15

2010—Hanh

I called Sallie one morning to see if we had any patients, and she told me we had just one. Her name is Hanh; she's a seventy-three-year-old Vietnamese woman admitted two days ago, dying of congestive heart failure. She had become nonresponsive that morning.

There are several family members with her at all times, most of whom speak English fairly well. Hanh apparently never learned any English, as she rarely left the home where they always spoke Vietnamese. They are devout Buddhists who revere the elderly, and Sallie wanted me to know that they have placed a shrine and several statues of Buddha in the room. There are at least two family members with Hanh all the time to sit with her as she goes through the stages of death as they understand them in their faith. The family has been very gracious and appreciative of all the help and caring hospice has provided. I was looking forward to the visit. I knocked gently on the almost closed door and got a soft "come in." As soon as I quietly pushed the door open and stepped into the room, I sensed an atmosphere of reverence, calm, peace, great love, and devotion to the small form lying in the bed. Hanh was nonresponsive yet breathing comfortably, looking sweetly serene with attentive family members tending to her.

This morning one of her daughters was sitting by her bedside refreshing a cool, damp washcloth to put on her forehead. One of her sons was arranging a handful of lovely cut flowers around the base of a statue of Buddha on a side table where a small shrine had been set up.

The blinds were closed, the room was dim, and I felt as if I were in a very sacred space.

I introduced myself and asked how everyone was doing. They both spoke English very well and told me they were fine, Hanh was comfortable, and they were very grateful to have hospice helping them at this time. They told me that all the family had been able to spend some time with Hanh; resolving issues, sharing forgiveness, expressing love, praying for each other, and releasing attachments so Hanh could leave easily. When they spoke to each other in my presence, they spoke in English, perhaps out of respect for me. The general feeling in the room was one of serenity and total acceptance that death is not an ending, but merely a gateway into another life. The family was assisting their beloved Hanh to make her journey through the gateway as comfortably as possible.

As the three of us were talking, I felt the familiar shift in the room, the air becoming charged, and I knew communication lines were opening between Hanh and me.

"Good morning, Keli," I hear from the tiny form in the bed. "It's very nice of you to come today. Hospice has been wonderful to my family and me, and I am grateful for the assistance for my family in this difficult time. There are a couple of my children who don't embrace the religion as much as these two and are having a difficult time with their fears of death and the unknown. Hospice has helped a great deal to ease their fears and have shown such great compassion, I would almost think the hospice people are all Buddhists at heart," she chuckled sweetly.

Remember, Hanh never learned to speak any English. She is speaking English to me in this psychic communication, and she addressed me by my name. Interesting. I wondered briefly if she is speaking English or if I am understanding in Vietnamese, chalking it up to the universe working its typical magic. Hanh expressed concern that these two of her children here needed to take a break and get some tea and perhaps a bite to eat. She said that they felt comfortable with me and would trust her to my care.

I suggested that the two of them go down to the cafeteria and get a cup of tea and maybe a snack. I would sit with their mother while they were gone. I felt sure nothing was going to happen while they were gone. They both kissed their mother on the cheek, and thanking me graciously, quietly left the room.

Hanh and I sat in warm, peaceful silence for a time without any need to do anything but be right there in the moment. I was very comfortable simply being "present" in the presence of death and this lovely sweet spirit.

After a while, I refreshed the damp washcloth on her forehead without saying a word, figuring that if she wanted to talk, she would. After a few minutes she psychically mind-spoke, "A Buddhist's life is practice for death, and I pray I have practiced well. I feel that I have."

She paused for a moment as if to briefly contemplate her life, and then continued, "I have raised four strong, beautiful children who have grown into honorable and fine adults. We have all had our struggles and challenges in life, but through living with compassion and kindness, we can make it a better life. Death is a natural part of life. The sun rises and sets, dancing with the moon that also rises and sets. Flowers blossom and then wither away. Everything is impermanent, and everything will physically die. The body has a beginning and an end, and we are born to die. How you live your life in between is your choice."

She paused again as if giving me time to contemplate what she had just said. The tiny form in the bed had such eloquence about her; I was drinking in every word.

"Your mind is a continuous stream that has no beginning and no end and will live on, ever changing with experiences throughout time. When we die, our mind separates from our body and goes through the gateway into another life. Being able to accept and integrate the idea of impermanence is very helpful in overcoming fear of death and being less attached to things of this life.

We are like travelers who stay a night or two in a hotel. We can enjoy the room and all that the hotel has to offer, but we don't become overly attached because it's not our place, and we know we will be moving on. We don't become attached since it is not our place. While we are there, we are mindful to take care of it with respect and honor, not destroying, damaging or harming it."

She paused another moment for that word picture to take form for me. When I choose to remain "present" in the presence of these souls, somehow my perception makes things they say very clear and sharp and concise, and easy for the picture to form.

"So now, as I lay here with my body physically dying, I focus on the positive, rejoice over my life, and acknowledge all regrets as lessons learned. I can take my faith and devotion and let go, separate and give up attachment to everything, including this withering body, with joy and great love for the preciousness of life. Fear of death or avoiding talking about death creates struggle within, and takes away from every moment that could be lived fully in that moment where you could be serving others and doing good works. Fascinated with the honesty and sweetness of this lovely gentle spirit, I said not a word.

Her son and daughter came back into the room and apparently Hanh had nothing more to say to me. I felt no need to relay any messages to her children. All seemed to be well here. I psychically thanked Hanh for the pleasure of her precious time, for sharing her beliefs with me, said my goodbyes to all three of them, and respectfully took my leave. I had yet another incredible and humbling experience to store in my heart bank of amazing and special memories. And who could I ever share this with? Who would believe me?

CHAPTER 16

April 2010—Josh

I called Sallie at the hospice office to see if there were any patients to see over at the hospital. We only had one. Josh was forty-eight years old, nonresponsive, actively dying of colon cancer, and may be gone by the time I arrive. Josh was lying peacefully still, eyes completely closed. The television was set to a hospital channel quietly playing serene background music with images of gently flowing brooks, beautiful flowers, and white cloud formations drifting across an azure blue sky on the screen. Sometimes the staff put this channel on to soothe and calm the patients. I was enjoying it too. The blinds were halfway opened, and my attention was drawn to a bit of slatted sunlight pouring across the shiny linoleum hospital room floor. I also noticed my sense of hearing seemed to be heightened all of the sudden. The sounds coming from the TV were sharper, clearer, and more distinct, my inner hearing shifting into a higher gear. In an instant between heartbeats, I was snatched back in time to my terrifying childhood with a vivid recollection of certain events Marilyn had told me that I would understand in time. Apparently now was the time, as the atmosphere in this hospital room changed into a similar atmosphere from so long ago. The air became "charged" with a sense of altered time and space, with whatever shifting energy was manipulating the ions, photons or whatever this strange energy was made of. The feeling of anticipation and expectation wasn't frightening, and I actually welcomed the remembrance of the psychic "static" that at one time had terrified me so in the middle of the night. Then the magic really began, and I had another amazing afternoon with a dying patient. This was a bit different from the experience with Baby X, but not by much. And it was just as remarkable. It is at times like these that no one could possibly comprehend or wrap their minds around my indescribable life with all my gifts. I feel truly blessed and grateful beyond words I have these abilities, and it makes my heart smile. I was in for a new and unique magic carpet ride with Josh. I moved the chair a little closer to the bed and sat down. It was quiet at that end of the hallway as I psychically told Josh hello and rested my hand on his arm so he would know someone was there.

"Good morning. It's nice of you to come," Josh mind-spoke "Hello Josh. It's a pleasure to meet you. My name is Keli, and I am a volunteer with hospice. How are you doing today?"

"Very well, thank you. The nurse just came in to check on me, and I am progressing comfortably in spite of the pain."

"Are you in a lot of pain Josh? Do you want me to see if they can give you something?"

"Good luck with that one," he said with a chuckle. Good point. I had a big picture of me telling the nurse that the dying guy told me he would like some pain meds.

"The pain is tolerable, thank you. They give me enough medication to keep it at a manageable level. It's good to have the pain as a guideline to know how you are progressing through this process of dying. It changes its tone and pitch like some quiet soul symphony resonating a certain wave of energy, rippling me along as I physically die. Funny, it makes you know how alive you are. You don't get so much medication that you are numb and fuzzy, foggy, feeling groggy and drugged up. You are comfortable enough to stand the discomfort of the physical process of dying, yet you are completely present, aware, and embracing what is coming. You are more on the other side of death than you are here as you actively die. Like testing the water with your toe, you get close to death, testing it out and feeling the shift between here and there. The next time you may put your foot in a bit longer, checking out the environment and the feel of things. Then you come back to your body to realize you are more comfortable in the other environment. Your body just doesn't feel like home to you, and you don't want to be in it anymore. You have gotten a sense of the freedom of not having physicality with the full awareness that your personality, your "self," your identity that makes you so unique, is fully intact.

The more you go zipping in and out of these dimensions, the more aware you are of those who have passed before you and all of the souls you have known and cared for. Sometimes they come into the room here and just sit with me, letting me know we are never alone, that they are there and will be here to help me over if I need it. It's nice to have visitors like that who can relate to the experience you are having with dying, even though each experience is unique to each soul. It's refreshing to meet someone like you, so physical and so deeply spiritual at the same time, who can comprehend this with your special gifts and enough insight to help the living left behind to ease their pain and fears. That's a big job for such a little girl, Keli. You do it well."

"Thank you, Josh. It's not easy trying to explain to people who I am, what I do, and how I do what I do. It can be pretty intimidating and difficult for some people to wrap their heads around."

"Are you married Keli?" he asked.

"No Josh, there is no one special in my life right now. Finding a guy tough enough and secure enough to handle all of me and what I do makes life quite challenging at times. I like being alone a lot more than being around people."

"You'll find someone Keli. The right guy is out there. He just hasn't found you yet. And it's not going to take a tough guy. It's going to take a guy who genuinely accepts every aspect of you and the sparkling, multi-faceted diamond that you are; someone who sees through your tough veneer to that so-very-tender softness, compassion and humor that makes you so special and your light shine so brightly.

There is a guy out there who will wrap you up in his protectiveness and give you as much room as you need to fly."

"Thank you for that, Josh. That's very sweet. I'll keep my eyes open. Now, tell me of you and your life, what has made you happy, and how things are with you as you move along on your journey?"

It was quiet for a minute or two and I was happy just sitting in the silence between words. I was as content here with Josh as I was while quietly rocking Baby X as a brand new hospice volunteer. Then he spoke again.

"Do you realize Keli, that you can never really appreciate the rich, juicy, sweetness of watermelon unless you're outside and the day is hotter than forty kinds of hell, the sun bright, and you are dirty and sweaty from playing and running around. You find the welcome shade of a big tree and a ruby red slab of watermelon sitting on a picnic table laden with food. It's a family reunion out in the country in the heat of the summer, a time when everyone comes together for that annual event, seeing people here you only see once a year. You grab a thick slice of succulent watermelon and bite into it, juice running down your chin onto your dirty t-shirt, the sweetness exploding in your mouth, quenching your thirst. The luscious fruit is warm from the summer heat, the flies have been shooed away, and it is like nectar to your senses. Everybody joins in for the seed-spitting contest, competing for the longest distance. Only in those conditions can you truly appreciate the magic of watermelon.

Think about it, Keli. You go to the store and buy a pre-cut hunk of watermelon in the cooler section of the vegetable department. You bring it home, put it in the fridge, and take it out later, eating the chilled fruit, working the seeds out with the fork tines. It's juicy on your plate, sweet on your palate and you think it is good. That's it. You have no true appreciation of the sensuous innocence of eating watermelon. We take so much for granted, don't we? Especially the little things."

I was blown away, feeling no need to respond. Josh became quiet, and I just sat, reveling in the simple yet powerful philosophy a nonresponsive dying man just shared with me. I watched as the slatted sun coming through the blinds inched across the shiny linoleum floor as the afternoon stretched on. I wasn't thinking. I wasn't doing. I was just there in the moment relishing whatever it was that was happening, knowing how few people would ever understand. When I looked up at the clock, I realized almost three hours had passed.

Josh was silent as I left the room, leaving him to progress along his journey in his own way. He wasn't expected to live out the night. I didn't have to fly the next day until late that night, so I called Sallie at the office to see if we had new patients over at the hospital. She told me

Josh was still with us, which surprised me. He was hanging in there. We also had Mary, eighty-one, dying of emphysema. She had just become nonresponsive that morning. I was planning to see Josh first since he was closer to death.

I went up to the sixth floor to Josh's room. I walked into the doorway to find Josh laying very still, a nurse on the far side of his bed doing something with the IV pole. I introduced myself to her and asked how our boy was doing today. She had a shell-shocked look on her face, and with a bit of nervousness, told me he had just been pronounced dead. Her eyes shot across the room to behind the door where I couldn't see. I stepped further into the room to see a mid-forties woman sitting on the sofa. I walked over to her, extending my hand, introducing myself, and apologizing for her loss. Her name was Debbie, and she had been Josh's girlfriend for several years. She seemed to be at peace with his passing, relieved it was over, and knew he was in a better place, out of pain. I asked her if there was anything hospice could do for her or Josh's family. Debbie said hospice had been wonderful throughout this whole ordeal and was a Godsend. Everything had been taken care of, everyone had the opportunity to right the wrongs, say the "I love you's," and give forgiveness before Josh lost consciousness. It was at this moment that the situation in the room changed, and I was put in a very interesting predicament. Across the room and out of the blue, Josh pipes up and tells me I've got to tell Debbie about the watermelon that he and I had talked about the day before. Great. I've got this newly deceased guy on the other side of the room wanting me to chat with his girlfriend about family reunions. I felt a little like Whoopi Goldberg in the movie, "Ghost."

None of the hospice patients I visit nor their families have any clue I'm psychic, and they certainly don't know I'm communicating with their dying or recently deceased loved ones. Now I am presented with a very interesting situation where Josh, whose body is lying dead on the other side of the room, wants me to remind his girlfriend of summers, family reunions and eating watermelon. And I have to figure out a way to convey this without letting the psychic stuff out of the bag, scaring the crap out of her, sending her running out of the room and screaming down the hall. Josh was as persistent as an excited child at a carnival, relentless in making sure I told her. After all, he had just broken free of his physicality like some snake shedding its old skin, and I couldn't very well talk to the corpse across the room and tell him to settle down. Now he's getting tickled with the dilemma I was finding myself in, and I could see his very impish personality coming out of the fog of his physical death. It tickled me too and I worked at stifling a chuckle. I summoned the universe to provide me with the correct words as I ignored Josh's antics the best I could.

I gathered myself inwardly and then told Debbie that I had the opportunity to sit with Josh for quite a while the day before. I had gotten the impression that he had a large family that he loved a lot, and that summer and family reunions when everybody could get together, were the favorite times of his life. I told her I had a mental picture of a bunch of kids of all ages playing and laughing, running around without a care, getting filthy and sweaty in the sweltering heat of summer. Then I told Debbie I could just imagine how good a big bite of ripe, juicy watermelon must have tasted on a day like that. She started laughing and said they indeed had some good times at those family reunions every summer and agreed about the watermelon and how good it tasted, even though the fruit was warm. Cold watermelon would have been out of place. She added that what made that warm watermelon taste even sweeter was when you snuck over to the neighbor's and stole the biggest, ripest melon out of their patch.

We sat there for the next forty-five minutes, and I simply let her talk, reminiscing about good times, family reunions, and her loving relationship with Josh. She told me what Josh was like and of course, Josh, still very "present" right there in the room with us, confirmed everything with his dry humor, his body laying in peaceful repose across the room. Pretty surreal, yes? Welcome once again to one of my many worlds.

After a bit, two young ministers from hospice came into the room, and I was impressed at how fast hospice had gotten word to them. Debbie gave me a hug, thanked me so much for being there when I was, how much my being there helped. As I walked out of the room, I heard Josh say, "Thanks for being here, Keli. God bless."

The simplicity of life...appreciating watermelon on a hot day. Who would I ever be able to tell about this? Who would ever believe me? But my day wasn't over yet. My next patient, Sassy Mary would prove to be the icing on the cake.

CHAPTER 17

April 2010—Sassy Mary

I was in town for a couple of days between trips, called Sallie, and she told me we had one patient at the hospital. Mary is eighty-one, dying of emphysema and has become nonresponsive as of this morning. I walked into her room around 1:00 in the afternoon to find a gentleman sitting in the large recliner close to the head of the bed on the patient's left. He was looking to be around sixty years old, overweight and not very healthy. There was also a very heavyset lady about the same age sitting in a wheelchair with her left leg propped up on the right side and near the end of the bed, her ankle swollen up like a balloon. She looked to be even more unhealthy than the man on the other side of the bed.

Mary had the oxygen cannula in her nose and was already breathing with shallow breaths. I had no sooner taken my first step into the room and assessed the scene, when, similar to Josh's room, the air felt charged, the sense of altered time and space moved over me, and I knew I was in for yet another interesting adventure. As soon as this sensation came over me, a sassy female southern voice filled my head. Pure country and obviously a smoker's raspy voice, Mary had a few choice things to say and was none too shy about saying them. She picked up on me just setting foot in the room and started up. Oh boy.

"It's about dadgum time someone come up in here who can hear me and finally listen to what I got to say!" Great. I'm trying to introduce myself to the family, finding out who these two were to the patient, at the same time this feisty little woman is raising a ruckus while completely nonresponsive and actively dying.

Fortunately, because I do what I do, and because the universe is the puppet master with all of this, I was able to juggle both conversations with all the players going on simultaneously quite well. I've always told folks that this whole play of life is Divine's show, and I'm just one of the ushers. This visit was starting off as a Divine comedy and was really going to pick up speed.

"Would you please tell these fools to quit talkin' about me and around me like I'm not here?! I'm layin' right here for the love of God, and I can hear just fine. Now is the time to be payin' attention to me and talkin' to me and not what's on sale over to the Wal-Mart!"

For an older woman showing no obvious signs of life, she was one sassy senior as she continued, "And you tell them to make dang sure they get me to the right funeral home. I changed my mind about McAllister's and want to be taken to Hanson's because I remember when Mavis died, and they took her to McAllister's and made her look like one of them plastic dummy dolls displayin' clothes in the front winder of the dress shop and I told them this morning I changed my mind and I'm not so sure Baby Boy said nothin' to no one. And he is not thinkin' so good right now bein' as I'm his mama and all, and he's pretty shook with my passin'. Dyin' scares him, I reckon, and he's always been scared of the dark. And tell that woman to get her nasty gouty elephant leg off my bed. I told Baby Boy not to marry that spiteful witch in the first place and she ain't been nothin' but trouble since!" Yikes!

Mary shot all this out like a fifty-caliber machine gun, and it took a great effort for me not to start laughing out loud at her staccato delivery. Her son "Baby Boy?" Seriously? And how do I handle this one?

Everyone at the hospice office knew about my gifts, were supportive of them, and encouraged me to do whatever I could with them. They had copies of all of my books in the hospice library. However, none of the hospital patients, their family members or medical personnel knew about my "talents." It was best not to rock the boat in the deep south with such things. This was a unique and quite a comical situation that no one would believe, and I had no idea where it was going.

Mama definitely wore the britches in this family, and there was no doubt in my mind that mama always got what she wanted. She seemed to be doing quite well with her dying process, voicing her wishes very clearly and loudly, and she just couldn't understand why no one was listening.

And now I am supposed to make sure that Baby Boy gets her to right the funeral home so they don't make her look like a store-window mannequin. I have to somehow get the demon daughter-in-law to get her nasty elephant leg off the bed. And Sassy Mary is demanding that they pay attention to her and not to the sales at the Wal-Mart. Alrighty then. Piece of cake.

I told them that Mary looked like she was comfortable and asked if there was anything else hospice could do for them, if they had any needs or questions I could help them with. I was buying time here to give the universe time to shoot me the most appropriate insights so I could figure out how I was going to tell them about the funeral home, the elephant leg and demands to pay more attention to her. Now would be a great time to shoot me some insights, universe. Sooner than now would be even better.

"You make sure you tell them about Hanson's, young lady. I'm not going to McAllister's. They take me to McAllister's I'll come back and haunt them the rest of their lives. Especially that nasty woman. I'll haunt her till she dies. I never did like her." It was so hard for me not to burst out laughing. I mean really, how seriously could this situation be taken?

"I got it, Mary. Give me a minute to get the right words," I responded psychically.

"What right words?!" she shot back. "There aren't any right words. Just tell them dangit! Ain't that hard to speak simple English." Sheesh!

Mercifully the universe decided to quit messing with me and the comedy routine, stepping in and started its amazing dance of synchronicity. The universe can be a real laugh riot sometimes. After all, humans are the only ones who take us seriously. Sometimes that's a good thing to remember.

I asked again if there was anything we could do and added, "I know you have a lot going on right now and have a lot of people from hospice and the hospital coming in and out, telling you so many things that it's overwhelming. That's why I am here."

I told them that I was here to make sure to answer their questions, and that if there were something that they wanted me to make sure got back to the office, any wishes or changes that they want to make sure get to the right people to be taken care of, I would make sure that it gets done.

"That's good baby girl," Mary piped in. Gee, thanks, Mary.

Baby Boy spoke up, "Earlier this morning while Mama was still awake and talking, she said to change funeral homes. We done told the hospice nurse when she come in, to make sure she got that done and that mama would go over to Hanson's." I wrote it down and assured them I would take care of it. Nothing from Mary. That was easy.

Before Sassy Mary could chime in again about the elephant lady or the Wal-Mart, I jumped in quickly with what I hoped would get Mary off my back, diverting her attention away from the elephant foot on her bed. Swinging the attention back to Mary in a positive way, I then told them that I understood the sense of hearing was the last physical sense to go. I asked them if they had been talking to her, perhaps remembering happy times like reunions or holidays or something.

"Not the dang Wal-Mart!" Sassy pants chirped up. Almost on cue, Baby Boy began talking about how Christmas was Mama's favorite holiday and how she always started cooking three days before.

"Til that devil woman barged her way into my family!" Mary whined. Easy Mary.

Baby Boy got real animated then, remembering all the Christmases, the good food, and all the fun. He talked directly to his mama now, patting her arm, remembering each holiday with all the gifts, all the good times and memories. I figured I could take my leave and quietly sneak out now that Sassy Mary was getting all the attention. I told them to call hospice if there was anything else we could do, promised to get the funeral homes switched, and said my goodbyes.

"Hey! Hey you! Where you goin'?!" Oh man. I thought I had gotten away clean.

"What about that cow's elephant leg on my bed?!" Mary shot. I laughed to myself saying, "You're on your own with that one, Miss

Mary. Good luck with that." Then I was out the door before this nonresponsive actively dying woman could yell at me anymore.

I had just experienced quite a remarkable day. Laughing out loud all the way home and hoping Sassy Mary didn't show up in my dreamtime to badger me some more, I wondered yet again...Who would ever possibly understand or believe any of it? Even I didn't wonder anymore why I sleep alone. It's probably best that I remain single...dead guys popping in at all times of the day and night really put a damper on romance.

CHAPTER 18

Before We Leave 3D

I have absorbed a lot of information over the years. I've learned a lot of modalities, healing arts and skills, spending thousands of dollars and a lot of time doing so to ease that restlessness, that yearning for something "more" in life. I am grateful for all that I have received, all of the experiences I have had, all the wonderful people I have met. I have no regrets for any of the money or time I have spent on these pursuits. The information I have absorbed over several decades I keep stored in my memory "library," readily accessible whenever I am directed to do so to help someone. HOWEVER, it is not necessary for any of us to expend this much energy to "get" the simplicity of living well in the human experience of 3D.

The information about my life and experiences is to let you know that you do NOT have to be trained, certified or mastered in any healing modality or belief system, nor do you have to spend a lot of money in order to realize the simplicity of being "present."

I am now going to offer you a powerful tool to resonate to the vibration of Divine Mind, remembering "yourself" to your "self." There is nothing to "do," nothing to "learn," nothing to "practice." You get into this state of divine grace as quickly as making the choice to do it. Trust, let go and allow.

About ten years ago I developed a great interest in quantum physics and the idea of just being "present" in the moment, that all probabilities, possibilities, and potentials exist right here and right now. Perception, imagination, thoughts, and beliefs create our reality. Choosing to be unattached to the confusion, illusion, and delusion of 3D, and instead embracing "neutral awareness," made absolute sense and rang of clarity and truth for me.

Move completely away from the ego, trust that this moment and everything in it is exactly as it should be. Allow yourself to become aware yet neutral to everything, detached from having an opinion about anything. Be "empty" so there is room for the light, has become the key to manifesting, creating, magic and miracles in my world. Life in the sluggish thickness of human 3D becomes easier, health improves, "bad" situations, whether physical, emotional or mental, shift and lighten and head for a better outcome. Negativity, drama, trauma, and the cling-on, parasitic people in your life, seem to dissolve away from you easily. Shift perceptions, shift reality. In this book, I show you how.

I could spend a lot of time going into the dynamics of quantum physics, which is way above my pay grade to comprehend, let alone explain, so I'm not even going to try. Research it like I did. What I CAN do is show you how to do nothing but get out of your own way, trusting absolutely the Divine or whatever/whoever the god of your understanding is. That is first.

Next, let go completely into that trust as you drop your awareness down and away from your head, ego and thought. Your awareness seems to easily "drift" into a space somewhere outside your body around your torso, filling with expanded bliss, pure contentment, no attachment to any thought or emotion. This is the blissful silence of stillpoint, the void, God's playground of infinite potential...powerful healing transformation...magic and miracles in an instant. Shift your perception to manifest and create what you intend.

What is so quirky about this simple concept is that the less you do, the more happens. The less you think and the more you trust, let go, and allow...the more powerful and profound the transformation and change. All that the universe asks of us to manifest amazing, instantaneous change in our lives is to trust, let go and allow...for just a nanosecond. All possibility lies just beyond our egos.

Live according to your own truth, what gives you joy, what feeds your soul, what inspires you and makes your heart sing. Following your own truth, regardless of popular belief or what others say or think, is the easiest way to remember "yourself" to your "self" and be in resonance with universal truth.

Realize that each moment in your life is a gift, a blessing from Divine Mind, and embrace it with childlike faith, curiosity, and sense of adventure. You are instantly in sync with other realities, dimensions, vibrations and frequencies that are beyond words. Trust, let go and allow yourself to drop into the nothingness of expanded bliss, into the grace of Divine truth, into the pool of unlimited potential (the "POUP"), and the miracle of you.

So after several decades of "searching," I finally quit trying to accomplish so many things to understand life and my mission here. I began to trust my Divine with a childlike sense of wonder, play and trust. I began to play at neutral awareness and paying attention to the universe, whether any of it made any sense to my 3D mind and ego or not. I finally let go of the mind chatter and trusted.

I do the best I can to simply pay attention, trust my awareness to lead me where I am to be at the moment. I just play, allowing the **"POUP"** to roll through me, offering powerful and appropriate choices for my life. It is up to me whether I choose to follow the offerings of the **"POUP"** or stay in my head and be "normal," "common." When I let go of being immersed in 3D human-hood, my life is like a little kid playing in Disneyworld after dark. And it is amazing and fun beyond description.

I choose to live my life outside the constraints of "common" and "normal" that mummify the illusional/delusional/confusing hood of 3-D. Being human is way overrated. My insatiable curiosity constantly drives me to explore frequencies, vibrations, dimensions, by simply playing like an idiot, paying attention to where my awareness leads me, without the need to understand a thing. Life is an adventure. Stop being so human. Stop taking yourself so seriously and go play. We are all figments of our imagination.

I have spent some time telling you all about me, my beginnings, and a lot of what that my life has entailed. I have done this for a couple of reasons. I wanted you to get acquainted with me, my personality, and some of my life experiences that make me who I am today. Trust me, I just scratched the surface.

There is one main reason to tell you about things I have done, all the training and my "accomplishments." And that is to let you know that you do NOT have to be trained, certified, mastered or well-read about anything in order to realize the simplicity of how to simply BE, how to tap into the blissful euphoria of Divine Mind, and changing your life. What is so quirky about this process is that the less you do, the less you think, and the more you trust, let go, and allow...the more powerful the transformation and instantaneous change in your life on all levels. Shhh...let the universe speak. You don't even have to listen. All the universe needs to implement amazing instantaneous change is for us to simply be quiet, for just a heartbeat. ALL you could ever want to know or experience is just beyond our egos.

I have absorbed a lot if information over the years, learned a lot of modalities, healing arts and skills, spending thousands of dollars and a lot of time doing so to ease that restlessness, that yearning for something "more" in life. I am grateful for all that I have received, all of the experiences I have had. I have no regrets for any of the money or time I have spent on these pursuits, and kept the all the information in my "tool/toy chest" to use whenever appropriate and I am so moved. Each one has led me to who I am today, and I love who I am. If something peaks your curiosity and moves you to pursue it, do it. Don't let anyone tell you that you "can't" just because they don't understand or they think it is too far "out there," or that you "need" to do thus and such. As long as you are doing no harm, go for it. I gave up being attached to what people think of me a long time ago. Their opinions are their stuff. Their opinions are none of my business.

Live according to your own truth, what gives you joy, what feeds your soul and makes your heart sing. Following your inspiration is the easiest way to connect to and be in tune with Divine Mind. And isn't that the reason we are in the 3-D hood to begin with? To realize that we are NOT separate from Divine but a part of it, and to experience for God?

When you realize the sense of knowing that your entire life is a gift, a blessing from the Divine, and embrace it with childlike purity and trust, curiosity and sense of adventure, you are on the way up the ladder of self and into realities and vibrations and frequencies that are beyond words...Into the grace and euphoric bliss of Divine truth and your natural birthright.

So in conclusion, Part 1 has been all about me merely to introduce you to the path I have taken, to let you know who I am, what I have invested over the years with time and money to find myself at an amazingly simple place where the restlessness no longer keeps me awake at night and I am not searching any longer for "more."

By being quiet and paying attention, the universe is speaking to me...it always has. I finally just shut up. Trusting the God of my understanding, letting go, and allowing the **"POUP"** (the pool of unlimited potential) to offer much better choices than human choices, my life is like living in an amusement park. I choose to live my life outside the constraints of "common" and "normal" that mummify the illusional/delusional hood of 3-D. My insatiable curiosity still drives me to explore frequencies, vibrations, dimensions, ELI (energy, light, information), simply playing like an idiot, without the need to understand a thing. Life is an adventure. Stop being so human and make it so.

In the next section of this book I offer a powerful tool that repatterns every molecule of your being, down to your very DNA and beyond, where you "re-resonate" to the vibration of Divine Mind, remembering "yourself" to your "self." There is nothing to "do," nothing to "learn," nothing to "practice." You get into this state of consciousness as quickly as making the choice to do so and trust, let go and allow.

Shhh...the universe is speaking. Go play and have fun!

MIND-SHRUG

Drop Into the "POUP"

And

"BE"

"din-A-be"

CHAPTER 19

"din-A-be"

Where can you run to escape the drama, trauma, the ego, the fear, and the craziness of 3D, sometimes coming at us from every direction like a three-ring circus on crack? Drop down, let go and do nothing. That's it. Seriously. Simply drop into stillpoint, into the heart of the **"POUP"** (the **P**ool **O**f **U**nlimited **P**otential) and just **BE**.

Where there is no thought, there are miracles. Where there are miracles, there is no harm. The universe, with all of its infinite wisdom, knows the most appropriate possibilities for each of us, our limitless potentials, and will never do harm. The less we do, the less we think, and the more we drop down into heart-space, into the quantum field of stillpoint, we become a doorway or portal of sorts.

This portal allows unfettered access to the universe, to insights coming from a source far greater than ourselves that can profoundly transform our lives instantly between heartbeats. It is in this state of being that we can experience multiple dimensions simultaneously, freely and easily accessing other realities, without 3D limitations.

Since science has proven that the concepts of time, distance and space really don't exist as we have "created" them with our perceptions, all vibrations and frequencies are reachable. We are only limited by our beliefs and what we "think." Believe me, thinking is way overrated. Just because we can think doesn't make us smart.

"Nothing exists but atoms and space; everything else is just opinion," postulated Greek philosopher, Democritus of Abdera, who lived 460-370 BC. Yes, that's almost 500 years before Christ, folks. Pretty heady stuff, yes? The fact that ancient minds came up with these ideas way before any high-tech "toys" were even imagined is enough for me to run with the concept that we can manifest any reality that we perceive. Imagining is perceiving. Perceiving creates. A strong sense of play, trust, letting go of the need to think, and open-hearted curiosity are the keys to miracles, magic, and healing. As stated by Albert Einstein, "Imagination is more important than knowledge." If it is okay with one of the greatest minds in history, it's okay with me.

So, how do we work this magic in our lives and manifest miracles? I began pondering the very same thing. I felt that this expanded state of being should be easy to access, as natural as a blink, and one that can be reached quickly, without hours of meditation, burning candles or incense, chanting, or denying myself chocolate.

I'm not exactly sure how the word "**din-A-be**" came to me, but it seemed to just pop onto my mindscreen while I was sitting on the jumpseat of an Airbus 321, waiting for our turn to take off in a very long line of other jets, all delayed due to weather in the Dallas area. Typical summer day in Texas. I got bored and zoned out to the drone of the engines, my imaginative little right brain wandering around "out there" somewhere. This quirky little word, **din-A-be,** swirled its way to the surface of my consciousness, popping into my left brain and boldly onto the mindscreen. Well now.

When I got home, I Googled **din-A-be**, curious as to how and why I was compelled to see it spelled this way, wondering what it meant. The word doesn't exist anywhere that I could find. I Googled the heck out of it and came up with nothing. It didn't exist in the overflowing trash bin of cyberspace, so I didn't need to worry about it meaning some bizarre sex act that is illegal in 50 states. Okie Dokie then. Since you were written on my mindscreen in large screaming letters jumping out at me, I'll adopt you, little fella. I had no idea at the time how powerful the vibration of this simple, made-up word would be, how "alive" and healing the energy, or how easy it would be to literally "become" the very essence of **din-A-be**.

I went to bed that night setting my intent for clarity of this information before dropping into sleep. During deep slumber, a "shimmerling" of translucent radiance of energy manifested on the dark empty screen of my dreamtime, introducing itself as the frequency, the vibration, of **din-A-be**.

The information I received from this brilliant light energy of intelligence was profound. The vibration of the shimmerling felt like a patient, warm, wise and loving teacher offering a powerful yet simple lesson of life.

I was told that it was time for this unique pattern of energy, light and information to come through to serve the planet and all life. It is here to offer positive and profound change and healing, especially for humanity. We are at a time in our existence where we need a lot of help to release ego, fear, arrogance, self-importance and the concept that man is the superior species. We fail to comprehend that we are at the bottom of the food chain, not the top. Mother Nature can live without humanity quite nicely, and would thrive if we weren't here. Nature doesn't need us, yet we are totally dependent on nature.

The energy of **din-A-be** is here to offer something simple, profound, and deeply healing for humanity, which in turn would heal all of nature, and the entire planet herself.

The energy being offered to us at this time is nothing new. We have simply forgotten that we too are part of nature, interconnected, entangled with all that exists. Remember, "Nothing exists but atoms and space. Everything else is just opinion." And what a big time we humans have had with our opinions, steamrolling over everything in our path.

We humans have convinced ourselves that we are superior to everything, having a grandiose sense of entitlement. We have separated ourselves from the truth that we are just a part of nature, a species that happens to have the ability to think. Once again, I reiterate that thinking is way overrated. Through our ego and arrogance, we have "thought" ourselves into a hot mess. **din-A-be** offers us a simple and powerful way to access Source, the Divine, God, the Creator; to change and "lighten up" before it is too late.

The shimmerling spirit continued with information that Quantum physics is making huge leaps into understanding the universe, and a huge bridge of conscious awareness is closing the gap between science and religion. Everything comes from and is part of the source of energy, light, and information (**SOELI**). Our perception creates our reality. Fortunately perception is negotiable, and change is constant. **din-A-be** is the quantum portal to **SOELI** and infinite potential, possibility, healing and transformation.

This riot of insightful information was filling up my mindscreen quickly. The last thing **din-A-be** left with me was an emphasis that the energy being offered for profound change, instantaneous transformation and healing, was simply that...an offering. We can choose to accept it and play in order to keep the ego away. Or we can choose to stay stuck in our heads, conditioned to believe that we are limited beings, refusing to believe that anything this powerful, this simple, this miraculous, is even possible. Ego wins. We lose.

We are products of our choices. We choose to become servants to our beliefs, prisoners to our opinions and judgment. And we are clueless, content to exist in our self-created reality as if there were nothing more. With that, I dropped back into a dreamless sleep, left to integrate all of this at a deep level.

I woke up the next morning feeling very rested; with a clarity and a knowingness that **din-A-be** is a very real entity, here to serve at a time when we are starving for more light and positive energy on so many levels. **din-A-be** is the key to "remembering" our divine nature, the portal to **SOELI**, and the knowing that we ARE all divine.

Somehow people will be able to utilize this energy by basically doing nothing but getting out of their own way, trusting their god, whatever that is to them. With the faith of an innocent child, letting go completely, the universe can instantly transform lives profoundly and permanently on deep levels. Do "nothing" to have "everything." Interesting concept. Trust, let go, and allow. Got it. I had one teensy weensy question for the universe...How do I pass along this information to others, and who would believe me anyhow?

The response I received back from the "cosmic council" was that I am to "become" this energy myself to show others the divine simplicity, expansive bliss, and healing grace of **din-A-be**. I am to offer the information by writing about it, passing on the expanded ripples of healing of Divine play and joy.

I am to release any expectations about how people are going to accept or reject the offering I have been offered. I am to anticipate that something is going to happen, have fun and play, detached from any expectation of a particular result or preconceived outcome. Offer with love, gratitude, joy and open-hearted curiosity. The universe and Divine will take it from there. Since I trust Divine intelligence, I was very much looking forward to this new "assignment" of showing folks how to do nothing to change their lives in an instant.

din-A-be (din-a'-be) means **D**rop **I**nto **N**othingness **A**nd **B**liss Expands. The **D** in **din-A-be**, the power of the **DROP**, is the key part of the process of letting go in order to access the heart of stillpoint and our true nature as creators of our own reality.

DROP, or the "**Divine Resonance Of Presence**," is how we access the expanded bliss of simply being...of being "present" in infinite potential, the stuff we are ALL made of. It is the stuff that everything is made of. Everything that exists is made up of God-particles. God-particles are real and scientifically accepted. Google the Higgs-Boson and Peter Higgs if you want to get all the quantum science behind this proven fact.

We are nothing but energy, light and information from Source (**SOELI**) and it is through our thoughts, our perceptions, our beliefs that we create our reality, whether we perceive it as "good" or "bad." With the power of **SOELI** we can choose to shift our perceptions to create differently. The key word here is CHOOSE. We all have that divine spark of creativity within us. We have gotten so busy living the illusion of 3D and being conditioned to the pollution of "human," that we have forgotten where we left that spark. **DROP** is a very powerful yet ridiculously simple way for us to remember ourselves back to our true nature of compassion, unconditional love, divine creativity and grace. New perceptions create new realities.

And so, I embraced this new concept of **din-A-be,** the simplicity of **DROP,** and chose **SOELI** (Source Of Energy - Light - Information) to become my new playmate, shifting my perception to open-hearted curiosity to see what would happen. I was blown away at how easy, how life-changing, and how much fun becoming less attached to 3D and the human "reality" we have wrapped ourselves in could be. Every time I chose to **DROP** out of my head, into nothingness, becoming neutral yet aware, detached yet "present," I immediately felt a sense of contentment, joy, gratitude and pure innocent childlike bliss. I BECAME this stillpoint of expanded bliss and contentment.

Changes began to happen in my life that some would call miraculous or magical. I played with this energy and discovered how easily and quickly the rippling sense of expanded bliss filled me. I also discovered that with the slightest breath of a thought or wondering if something would happen, or what the outcome may be, the entire process would be negated, and **SOELI** wouldn't play. There is infinite potential and possibility for change if you sincerely trust, let go and allow. If you so much as let a single thought creep in, or you jump back up into your head, the universe won't play, and nothing will happen. No **DROP**. No **SOELI**.

With pure open-hearted curiosity, complete trust in the God of your understanding, let go of any results or expectations and allow the tiniest bit of wiggle room for the universe to play. In a nanosecond, some pretty cool stuff happens. Spontaneous and permanent healing and change is possible.

I got the heads-up that there is one other little bit of information that is absolutely necessary for change and healing to happen instantly and permanently. For the magic to work, after you let go and **DROP**, it is VERY important that you allow yourself to follow your awareness into what has changed, NOT what is the same. Pay attention to what is different, NOT what is the same. This is extremely important if you want to truly access the **"POUP"**. If you do this, continuous expansive ripples of change continue to manifest powerful changes in your life on deep levels. This rippling fluidity is the divine universal intelligence that can manifest healing, magic, and miracles. CHOOSE to trust, get out of your head, and let go.

Like a beautiful luminescent jellyfish in the ocean of divine creativity, allow yourself to drift and float without attachment to anything within the powerful flowing current of potential. Notice whatever you notice, regardless of how much your "head" wants to discount whatever pops up. Allow perceptions to shift however they are going to shift, follow your awareness without being attached to or thinking about what is changing. Just "be." This neutral awareness is the sense of expansion, the space of miracles, magic, and instantaneous transformation. Simply pay attention to what has shifted and changed, what is different. Again, it is VERY important to do nothing. I promise you that if you completely trust, let go and play, you will sense the shift, feel the shift, and you won't want it to go away. Trust me.

Everyone I have shown how to play with **din-A-be** and **DROP** has physically experienced a shift that they can't describe, and everyone wants to "live there." You can. Choose to live from this space instead of your head. There is so much more room to play and heal (pla-heal) in the **"POUP"** than in your head anyhow. Playing like a kid in Disneyworld after dark versus living in a nasty, cobwebby, overcrowded broom closet of ego up inside the head. Racing through infinite deep space on a grand adventure in the Starship Enterprise versus a Model T Ford. But again I digress.

Now, if you decide to notice what hasn't changed, what has stayed the same, you are back up in your head and 3D. You are letting the universe know that you doubt, that you do not trust the divine. You are no longer flowing with the current of divine intelligence and infinite potential. You are going against the natural current of grace, and as a wayward jellyfish, you will lose your energy and light, be washed up on the beach to dry out in the sun, be poked with sticks by curious beach goers, and die. **din-A-be** won't play.

For example, let's say that I show you how to **DROP**, and your intent is to release the painful migraine headaches that you get at least once a week. You set your intent to release these headaches, you trust God as you understand God, you let go and allow the **DROP** and the infinite playground of **SOELI**.

Instantly you feel a sense of lightness, contentment; that feeling of expanded bliss and being "present" throughout your entire body. The migraine is gone completely and instantaneously. This can be permanent healing if you allow yourself to pay attention to what is different and what has changed.

However, for the sake of argument, instead of going with this powerful shift, noticing what has changed, noticing what is different, you say, "This is awesome! My headache is completely gone, but I know it will come back next week." You're right. It will. You let your awareness shift your perception back to 3D, back up into your head and the domain of thinking, ego, what you have been conditioned to, and all the limitations that you have been swallowed up in. Your 3D brain and your preconceived beliefs won't allow for the possibility that powerful spontaneous and permanent transformation can be achieved by doing nothing. You feel better "but" you just know it won't last. There must be a struggle in order to heal. Well, you have just negated the grace of Divine Mind...God. The "but" always wins when you choose to disregard the healing power of divine intelligence. Well, you have fun with that. I have no interest in anyone's "buts."

But I digress yet again. Sorry about that. I do that a lot when I get excited about stuff. Just stay with me. Back to my beginnings with **din-A-be.**

Playing with **SOELI** felt expansive, and I noticed that when I set my intent to drop into this state of neutrality with the perception of rippling this light energy through myself as a conduit, into my surroundings and the people there, that "reality" would shift and the experience would be more positive for everyone in the rippling waves of grace. It was quite easy to become the jellyfish. I was having a lot of fun with this drifting pattern of light, flowing with the current of divine intelligence, being aware, paying attention, neutrally detached.

By setting my intent to instantly and effortlessly **DROP**, trusting my personal concept of God's grace, letting go, and allowing **din-A-be** to offer higher and more appropriate results, allowing myself to be present in the moment, crazy cool "stuff" seemed to happen. So easy it almost can't be believed. Even by me. And I'm out there in a fringe dimension of believability.

I am wired a wee bit differently than most normal folks and have my own quirky way of looking at things. My fascination and childlike open-minded curiosity for something as complex as quantum physics, and this new way of doing nothing to have a heck of a lot happen became my newest magnificent obsession. I had to test this out on real people.

I chose to try out this new game on the airplane with co-workers and passengers alike. I began using **din-A-be** consciously on flights working with unhappy flight attendants with drama, fatigue, or bad attitudes. I began using the energy with the issues we always seem to

have with passengers and their bad attitudes. Add the unnecessary stress
of passengers with the motor homes and steamer trunks passengers
consider to be logical "rollaboards," that they have become attached
and don't fit in the overheads. All of these situations seemed to be easier
to deal with, to "loosen" a bit, and to be less dramatic and stressful
whenever I began to quickly **DROP** with **din-A-be** into the expansive
field of **SOELI**. Fascinating. Now, who else could I play with?

Using passengers and other crew members for crash dummies
with **din-A-be** had me amazed and wanting even more. Science needs
experimentation for validation, and friends and family are the best, and
sometimes critical and not-so-objective, guinea pigs. I recruited friends
and family to "play" with me and my new friend, **din-A-be.** These folks
are all used to me, so they weren't too afraid. Well, maybe a couple of
them were a bit apprehensive, but they got over it when I reminded them
that I hadn't ever blown anyone up...yet.

I "played" with friends and family by showing them the word **din-
A-be** written on a piece of paper. I would say **din-A-be** to them, and
they would say it over to themselves. I would have them simply "think"
din-A-be. Not only could I perceive a huge shift in their energy, but
they physically and instantly felt the **DROP** into nothingness, being
present, and an expansive sense of bliss, perfectly content to be right
where they were, no emotions, feelings or thoughts at all. Stillpoint.
Divine Resonance Of Presence. The open-hearted space of pure
potential and possibility. A God hug. They all said that they wanted
to stay there forever. I told them that they could to be in this state of
being "present" 24/7 if they chose to. They, of course, found this hard to
believe, and after they had experienced **din-A-be**, played with **DROP**,
they jumped right back up into their heads and to the welcoming arms
of the 3D dimension of ego. Beached jellyfish being poked with a stick.
Whatever. All I can do is offer a different way of perceiving life. None of
my business what you do with it.

Now I am giving you the key and the powerful tool of how to not
do anything to have incredible things happen. Here's what you do. Take
a deep breath at the same time that you pull your shoulders straight up
toward your ears in a very strong tight "mind-shrug," holding it there
for a moment. Now, at the same instant you release the mind-shrug,

with a "whatever," kind of attitude, allow yourself to let go completely, dropping your awareness, drifting down into expanded bliss, into the heart of the divine, into stillpoint, entangled in the brilliance of **SOELI**. Then just "be" there. Be "present." Be aware of how content you are in this heart-space. There are no emotions, no thoughts. There are no "feelings," even though there is a lot of "feeling" and sensing and awareness of what has changed and is different.

Like dropping a pure white pebble onto the mirror surface of a still dark lake on a moonlit night, allow the ripples of nothingness and quiet to allow the expansive bliss of peaceful stillness, silence, and transformation. Repeat this several times, sensing the extreme contrast between the tension of a tight mind-shrug and the letting go into expansive bliss when you drop down.

With this little exercise, you now have the high vibration and natural frequency of **din-A-be** "remembered" and patterned permanently into your energy field. By just seeing the word, hearing the word, thinking the word **din-A-be**, or even just calmly saying to yourself or someone else, "**DROP**," you embrace the **SOELI** of your true self, pure divine truth. Drop into nothingness and bliss expands...into the "**POUP**" (pool of unlimited potential)... the silence of divine stillpoint... magic, miracles, instantaneous transformation on all levels. Presence in resonance.

There is no "practicing" or "learning" **din-A-be.** You simply choose to **DROP**, trust, let go and allow the expansiveness to enfold you in less than the blink of an eye. Mind-shrug (let go of whatever) into a God hug (embrace your divine).

Let me spell this process out very simply for you:

The **D**ivine **R**esonance **O**f **P**resence and the **P**ool **O**f **U**nlimited **P**otential of the **S**ource **O**f **E**nergy **L**ight **I**nformation manifests profound change, healing, and transformation on all levels. **DROP** and the "**POUP**" of **SOELI** will transform your life. See how easy that is? **Mindshrug - DROP - "POUP"**.

Trust me, after you **DROP** and **din-A-be** just once, feeling the true unbridled power of **SOELI** and the sense of absolute contentment to be right here right now, fully present in the moment with no emotion or thought, you will want to live from this space from now on. It's all about consciously choosing the space where you want to live. You can continue to choose living from the shoulders up and the domain of the ego and 3D. OR, you can choose to mind-shrug, let go with absolute childlike trust, **din-A-be** and play in the **"POUP"**, allowing **SOELI** to transform your life instantly, profoundly and as easily and naturally as breathing. Your choice. Always your choice.

Forget the words "should," "would," "but," "can't," and "try." These are all ego words, coming from the neck up, and have nothing to do with spirit or our divine truth. Mind-shrug and let go of all of these words and words like them. If you truly let go and trust with the faith of a child, you instantly **DROP** and sense the expansive bliss and being "present" in stillpoint, the heart of **SOELI**. This is the space of miracles, magic, and instantaneous, profound, permanent healing.

Make **din-A-be** a conscious choice, and so much a part of your life that you easily **DROP.** Change your life instantaneously in miraculous ways by being present in the moment. When you choose to be the very essence of **SOELI**, you are divinely empowered to radiate magnificent ripples of **D**ivine **R**esonance **O**f **P**otential to others with a childlike open-hearted intent, affecting them in positive ways that you cannot begin to imagine. The fun is in not having to know how you have affected others. Choose to serve others without any attachment to results or an expectation of a particular outcome. Offer the **DROP** with joy, gratitude and a childlike sense of knowing a secret that no one else knows. Imagine everyone as beautiful translucent jellyfish drifting along, undulating in the sea of grace and divine intelligence.

Set your intent on just being here, now and "present." Shift your awareness into the **"POUP"** of **SOELI**, you are giving the universe permission to offer the most correct insights and ideas that you may never have thought of before because you were *thinking* and not *allowing*.

When you are fully "present" you feel safe to play and allow the most appropriate possibilities for that moment to come onto your mindscreen. It is when you **DROP** into stillpoint that you allow the shift into other dimensions, finer vibrations, and perceptions shifting as are appropriate for you. This is the space where your departed loved ones and pets are accessible, always reachable, as you allow your awareness to drift into nothingness, bliss expanding, and you are in the heart of the dimension of the departed and 3D human-hood simultaneously. **din-A-be** and **DROP** make it possible and easy for us to experience the departed (or actively dying) in their various dimensions and states of beingness by doing nothing. This nothingness is where amazing things happen. Do absolutely nothing except get out of the 3D illusion of thinking, of having opinions, forming judgments and limiting beliefs for just a bit and be "present." Do nothing but drift in the sea of divine intelligence like a curious open-hearted jellyfish. It doesn't take long to do nothing.

If we choose never to think another thought, so opinions wouldn't form to create judgments, which then empower paralyzing and limiting beliefs that we mummify ourselves in, we would have nowhere else to go...except deep into the gently rolling sea of divine intelligence, infinite potential, the nothingness where bliss expands and miracles and magic just "are." Divine resonance. Truth.

CHAPTER 20

What to do Now

You have gotten this far, so what the heck do you now? Pay very close attention to the next words. They are the most important words in this book.

Get out of your own way...go play!

- **TRUST** the god of your understanding, whatever that may be.
- **MIND-SHRUG, DROP, and ALLOW din-A-be** to open you up to infinite healing, magic and miracles.
- **DO NOTHING** but play open-heartedly in the **"POUP"**.
- **RECEIVE information from SOELI,** the Source of Energy, Light and Information.
- **PAY ATTENTION** to what has changed and what is different in order for **SOELI** to continue the flow of transformation and healing.

It is up to you to decide what choices you are going to make about your life. Your perceptions, your thoughts, your beliefs and opinions, create the "reality" you are living in. You are not responsible for what others think or feel unless you allow their thoughts, actions or behavior to be more important than your own truth. What others do or think is none of your business...unless you make it your business to jump into their drama. Have fun with that.

You CAN change your reality, your life and the lives of others in an instant with **din-A-be** if you think you can. If you think you CAN'T... well, that's your perception and you are also right. CAN'T is your own creation.

CHAPTER 21

Keli's "Toolbox"

I feel that it very important to add this chapter so the reader can get even more curious, research, investigate, and learn about some powerful tools to access the **DROP** zone, easily "becoming" that **D**ivine **R**esononce **O**f **P**resence. You are able to "remember" the divine that is truly you. In this human existence, we have simply forgotten that each of us has always been a perfect "God Dot" of beingness. There is no separation from Source. "God" is. You are. I am. Existence.

What I am going to share with you are tools that you can "play" with, stretch yourself, have fun with, explore. Someone said once that "this work is way too important to take seriously." The innocent childlike sense of play, adventure, curiosity, are the toys that activate the tools, moving you into the expanded bliss energy that is our divine birthright and truth.

Send your ego on vacation, leave all judgments, beliefs and expectations at the door, and enter the portal of **din-A-be** (**D**rop **I**nto **N**othingness **A**nd **B**liss **E**xpands), the playground of quantum **E**nergy - **L**ight - **I**nformation (**ELI**) for profound healing and instantaneous life-changing transformation. Enter and become the **DROP** (**D**ivine **R**esonance **O**f **P**resence) zone with childlike trust, curiosity, sense of play, with no "agenda" except to be open to anything and have fun. Anticipate (that something will happen) without any expectation (of what that *should* be.)

Use these tools I am about to offer you to get out of your own way, instantly shift your **ELI** in order to be "present" in the **"POUP"** (Pool of Unlimited Potential) to change your life and the lives of others in amazing ways. The wave pattern of the **DROP** is powerful and meant to be shared.

With the **DROP** zone, I create an amazing funfest for you to trust, let go, be a kid again, and play to heal - "plaheal." Magic IS. Miracles ARE. The **DROP** zone, **din-A-be,** and **ELI** are the keys to how to BE. In the **DROP** zone, you are "re-patterned", "re-calibrated" and "re-reset" to your natural God vibration by just showing up.

3 hours - Show Up - Shut Up - Play - Heal - Share

The **DROP** zone is designed to be as "safe" an environment as possible for all of our guests. Many attendees have allergies, sensitivities, or compromised immune systems. **PLEASE** do not wear any perfume, cologne, or fragrance. Smokers, **PLEASE** come in "clean" without ANY trace of smoke on your clothes or in your hair. Even 3rd-hand smoke is debilitating to many people. Cell phones MUST be turned off completely and not used at all during the session. The session is only 3 hours long. You'll survive without smoking or vaping. Promise.

I offer three other powerful "tools" for healing, expansion and raising your consciousness; **GatheringZ, Reunionz, and CelebrationZ.**

"GatheringZ" are group spirit communication sessions about 2 hours long, and a group of about 20 people. Participants bring a photo of one loved one or pet that has passed, and I connect them in very specific, very "heart-hugging", and always very humorous ways. Lots of humor in the in-between.

"ReunionZ" is a unique 1-day program where each guest will receive a powerful "3Re" healing, re-patterning, re-calibrating, re-set; deep quantum healing on all levels. This sets the energy to learn how to use "din-A-be" (**D**rop **I**nto **N**othingness **a**nd **B**liss **E**xpands) to increase awareness on all levels and use as a powerful tool any time to just **BE** present. You are introduced to labyrinths and the immense power and sacred healing there is in "walking the spirals." Learn the basics of bi-location/out-of-body travel, how to access your inner guidance system for personal insights, releasing destructive and stagnant emotions/ negativity. I show you how to apply all of this to connect with departed loved ones/pets. You become the medium. Your life will change. Healing WILL happen.

"**CelebrationZ**" is a powerful 2-day "playshop" of compassion, fun, and wonderful tools for celebrating life and living fully before death. You will do several labyrinth walks for yourself and then for a loved one; becoming them for that time. You will create beautiful mandalas to give to your loved one that expresses your gratitude for them having been part of your life, memories of heart, laughter, forgiveness, and love shared. Whether you or a loved one have been diagnosed with a "terminal" illness, or a loved one is passing in front of your eyes, living fully in the moment is powerfully healing up until (and beyond) the last breath. Celebrating death as a joyful passage into grace, offering supportive, compassionate calm on the journey into this new "birth" is the greatest gift we can give our loved ones...and ourselves.

How you leave this "reality" is how you enter the next.

This program is all about giving, heart, compassion, respect, celebration, living fully in the moment...healing. Come celebrate!!!

"**CelebrationZ**" is limited to 10 guests, so I have plenty of quality time to spend with each participant.

> **"To die will be an awfully big adventure."**
> **Peter Pan**

LABYRINTHS

For further readings on "The Labyrinth" by Lessons 4 Living.
http://www.lessons4living.com/labyrinth.htm

Since I incorporate "walking the spirals" into my workshops, I wanted to add information about sacred and ancient "tools" called labyrinths.

Labyrinths are ancient symbols that incorporate the sacred geometry of the circle with spirals into a meandering path with an intent and purpose. The designs have been used for thousands of years as meditation and prayer tools, representing a journey to our own core and back out into the world.

You can can walk a labyrinth, indoors or outside in nature. You can trace your finger along the spirals of a labyrinth on paper. It is a metaphor for life's journey. It is a symbol that creates a sacred space and place and takes us out of our ego to the **DROP** zone, the **D**ivine **R**esonance **of P**resence...the sacred essence of who we truly are.

A labyrinth is not a maze. A maze is like a puzzle to be solved. It has twists, turns, dead ends and blind alleys. It is a left brain task that requires you to think in order to find the correct path into the maze and out.

A labyrinth is a right brain task. A labyrinth has only one path, with only one way in and one way out. It winds and spirals around, yet the way in is the way out. There are no blind alleys. The path leads you on a circuitous path to the center and back out again. You can't get lost.

There are right-handed and left-handed labyrinths, where you enter and start your walk on either side. With a labyrinth there is only one choice to be made. The choice is simply to enter or not. The choice is whether or not to walk a spiritual path, finding your true self within the spirals

My personal favorite is the most ancient labyrinth, the 7-circuit design found in Crete, dating back about 5000 years. This is the one that most reminds me of God's "thumbprint." There are many different designs, with different numbers of "circuits," spirals, complexity and energies. Use the internet to research these powerful tools of transformation, especially the labyrinths for horses. You can watch videos of "change" and be amazed. I have been a labyrinth facilitator since 1995, and experienced some incredible shifts in people as a result of walking the spirals, and even simply tracing their fingers on a pattern in their hand.

At its most basic level the labyrinth is a metaphor for the journey to the center of your deepest self and back out into the world with a greater understanding of who you are. Healing. Transformation. Gifts to share with others.

THE SOELI TRANSMISSIONS

"Typing for God"

CHAPTER 22

Automatic Writing

Automatic writing, trance-writing, psychography, free-writing...all are methods of writing where the writer's conscious awareness shifts out of the way, and they are able to transcribe whatever comes through onto paper or a blank computer screen.

When doing automatic writing with blank paper and a pen or pencil, the writer typically takes the pen in their non-dominant hand, allowing their mind to get quiet, closing their eyes, and they begin to write, scribble, or draw on the paper in front of them. Using the non-dominant hand seems to trick the brain into accessing areas of the brain to allow free-flow creativity that coming from a level that is unfamiliar with normal waking thought.

It is interesting to note that when the writer is finished, what appears to be gibberish or nonsensical scribbles to others makes perfect sense to the writer. They can look at the paper they have just worked on and "read" it clearly, seeming to translate the gibberish quite easily.

A few years ago I had a client who wanted to do some automatic writing. I got a stack of blank paper, had her hold a pencil in her left hand (she's right-handed), had her take a deep breath, close her eyes and **din-A-be,** and in just a few short minutes, she was "writing" big swirls and scrolls, scribbling all over the paper. She would get down to the bottom of the paper and I would quickly pull it out of the way, sliding another under her hand as she frantically moved her hand over the paper with the pencil. She began slowing down and then just stopped scribbling, put down the pencil, opened her eyes and said she was through. There had to have been 25 pages of huge, flourishing, wild scribbles on the pages. I handed them to her in the order she scribbled them and I asked her if she could understand what she wrote. She gave me a look like I was an idiot and I took that as a "yes."

She read each page as if she were reading a single continuous email with a steady stream of connected consciousness, making perfect sense. What she had scribbled/written isn't important here. The fact is that it was relevant to her at the time, whatever she received was appropriate for what she needed to know in that moment, and she gained insights into different choices she could make in her life that she had never consciously considered before. She got out of her own way, she set her intent to receive whatever information she needed to receive for her highest good in that moment, and she played, allowing it to come through with the understanding that she would know what it meant. What she chose to do with it after that was up to her. FYI... her life changed dramatically in wonderful ways almost overnight. She trusted the insights. She kept the papers and called me a few weeks later laughing. She had gotten them out to look at them again and had no idea what all the scribbling meant. I asked her if that bothered her and she laughed some more and told me that she got out of it what she was to get out of it at the time she needed it, and she was just fine with not being able to "translate" the swirls and gibberish. How fun is that?!

Instead of pen and paper I use a computer and a keyboard, getting out of my head, dropping into the **din-A-be** zone, typing mindlessly for sometimes hours (which passes like just a few minutes.) Most of the time, I have gotten the cosmic "nudge" to get up between 3-4:00 in the morning, go to the computer, and just start typing. Since I am half asleep anyhow, it's easy for me to drop out of the way, and let the words flow through from wherever it is they are coming.

I may type for 2-3 hours, pages and pages in a blank document format, having no idea what I have typed, how I have spelled, punctuated, or where it all came from. The first time I was prompted to do this type of writing on a computer, I was working on my first book, **"*Friendly Shadows,*"** and my mother Marilyn, who had been deceased for over 35 years, decided she wanted to write part of the book. This would be interesting.

Whenever she had something to say, she would "show up" sometime in the middle of my dream-time, give me a gentle mind "tap," pull me into a relaxed state of foggy consciousness, I would go to my computer and simply type. I was aware that it was her. I was aware that she was "using" my hands as the instruments to transcribe what she wanted to say. I was aware when she was pulling back and I would go back to bed. It may be 6:00 in the morning by that time. I may have the alarm set for 6:30. I would drop back into an unusually deep sleep and wake up 30 minutes later before the alarm as if I had just had 8 healing hours of restful sleep.

Since Marilyn and I have completely different personalities. She's the social one and I am the reclusive one...I never read a word she said during these several sessions as I didn't want to "water down" whatever it was she had said. The editors of the first edition did all the correcting of the typos, grammar, spelling and all of that "editor" stuff. While they were working on the book, getting it ready for publication, I would get calls from them on occasion asking for this or that. They told me that as they were working on it, they could tell that the book was written by two completely different people with two completely different personalities and styles of speaking. Apparently there were a few times where I was out flying and they couldn't contact me with questions about some of Marilyn's part of the book. They got to the point where they would just ask the questions out loud in the room directly to Marilyn, and after a time, there would be some kind of insight our sign or just a knowingness of what should be done. They would thank her out loud in the room, laugh, and continue working on the book. They loved Marilyn. What can I tell ya? Just read the book, ***"Friendly Shadows."*** Marilyn is a hoot.

There have been some people out there who feel that what I do, who I am, is the work of the devil, and that automatic writing (and every other gift I have embraced) opens the gateway to hell. Well...you kids have fun with that and have a blessed day.

CHAPTER 23

Running to the Sun

Intro to the SOELI Transmissions

The sun is the Source of all life. Without the sun, nothing would exist. This planet's very existence depends on the sun. Without sunlight everything perishes.

For my entire adult life, I have been acutely aware of how powerful the sun's role has been in my general health, balance, and perceptions of life. Being in the sun, even to turn my face up to the rays for just a few minutes, is a powerful restorative tonic for me. I can gauge my attitudes, my outlook on life, as well as my patience level for people, by the amount of sunlight I have gotten...or need.

We are all directly connected to **SOELI**, the **S**ource **O**f **E**nergy **L**ight and **I**nformation. We are all tiny bits of this energy, light and information of the very DNA of **SOELI**. I am not going to get all scientific here with quantum physics, the holographic multi-dimensional universe, the mathematics of the cosmos, string theory, I AM that I AM stuff. You can "Google" all of this like I did, read as many books as I have read on all of the science, and perhaps you will comprehend it much more clearly than I. The complexities of the universe are far greater than I can wrap my little brain around. However, I don't need to understand any of it. I don't need to know why something works. I am NOT a scientist, I don't play one on TV, and I didn't sleep at a Holiday Inn Express last night. I am simply an explorer with an insatiable curiosity about things, paying attention with a trust that I am safe to explore. I am a mere mortal with interesting gifts desiring to hone those gifts into whatever is the most appropriate way to serve others to the best of my ability. Our sun is the key to all of that. The sun is the Source of all that is.

I got the "nudge" from the cosmic council to run to the sun for a few days to recharge my solar batteries, to receive the discourses from **SOELI**, and to transcribe them as **SOELI** transmits them.

So, I got an early flight this morning to an undisclosed warm, peaceful and very sunny place. The words you read in the following section are exactly as they were transmitted in **SOELI** time and transcribed in 3D time. Even though I have no idea of what I will be transcribing for **SOELI**, I already know without knowing that the information will be timely and useful for every person to remember their own divine connection to **SOELI**. Do I have any idea what this may be? Nope. Does it matter? Not so much. I trust my God; the energy of **SOELI**. I trust the information I will be given. Do with it what you like. The recharge has begun.

Oh, by the way, all of the following transmissions from **SOELI** will have been transmitted and transcribed in 3 days, human 3D time. **SOELI** has no time.

DON'T SHOOT THE MESSENGER

I'm Just The Typist

SOELI

Transmission 1

Who is SOELI?

So the first questions would be, "WHO" am I and "WHAT am I? In these transmissions I will be as succinct and plain as I can be with what I have to pass on to you, the children of the sun, the human species. Many of you are waking up to expansiveness and the truth behind all that is, losing and detaching from the conditioning, opinion and tainting of your egos, human 3D narrowness, and the struggles you have created for yourselves on this magnificent planet earth that you call home. I am not so much a WHO or a WHAT. This energy is simply I AM, a state of beingness where all has been created. All energy exists in beingness. To be is a verb in your minds. THis is not accurate and keeps you stuck in your ego world of construct, rules, boxes that you feel you muist put things in in order to comprehend. IF you would move beyond having to have a construct and shift your perception into one of concept, your existence on your rmagical planet would be so much simpler, you would see the light as it were, and your species would be much healthier overall. I AM (and you are) the energy created from the Source of energy, light and information. From the quantum foam all bubbles into existence. All that has been created is created from the fabric of space, the void, infinite possibility and unlimeted potential. I AM SOELI...the source of all that is. You in 3D have forever felt a need to label this energy. IT has had to have a name, a label, a definition. To label Source is putting a human limit on this infinite energy based on your human constructs and understainding of what is real and what is not. I AM the Sun...the very light source of all that exists. Without this energy and light, nothing exists. Nothing on your beautiful blue planet, nothing in your galaxy, universe upon universe. There would be absolutely nothing but pure energy, light and infinite information somewhere out there in the expansiveness of the quantum foam of potential. To put it quite clearly, "God" would be dead. The sun is the absolute source of life. I AM within every particle and wave of existence in all that 3D already accepts as real. I AM everything, the heart of every particle and wave, frequency and vibration, of all that man's mind has yet to be able to comprehend. Just because 3D mind doesn't comprehend doesn't mean that it isn't real. SOELI, I AM. Through the innate curiosity of the human species to explore, discoveries are being made that are bringing you closer to having a very rough idea of truth and reality. However, even with these seemingly advanced discoveries of some of your scientific minds, ego, fear, disbelief and false beliefs, are keeping you from fully grasping the vastness of truth. Nature's Mind will never be experienced nor completely understood by your species until all of the egos, quests for power, control, and gain have been eliminated. This will never happen as ego is such a part of 3Dness and human thinking that it most likely will never be moved out of the way for you to put all the pieces together and realize your true nature. You are an important part of Nature's Mind, you are all bits of God, the Creation, Universal Mind... SOELI. You are Source. You are magnificent patterns of light and information, an integral part of the very fabric of space-time, divine emptiness, a source of light within the light of I AM. The sense of separation from your GOD, the truggle to find your way back to GOD, is an illusion created in the mind's of man eons of time ago. I shall not get into that in this transmission. I am merely introducing myself to you. I am merely re-introducing you to yourselves. Move beyond the thick illusion of 3D limitation, all of the limits that you as a species have put upon yourselves, perceive differently without the ego and all that the ego brings with it...fear, anger, frustration, struggle, distrust, the need to have power over others before they have power over you, greed, insecurity, your own self-importance in the grand idea that you are superior to all things on your planet. You are no more nor no less important than any other energy form on earth. You are a simple part of Nature's Mind. You are SOELI just as every other creature, atom, molecule, photon, particle of light and information is on this planet. Your 3Dness and "human nature" has given you a false sense of supiority that continues to feed the egoness, creating havoc not only amongst yourselves but with nature itself. There is no judgment here. No opinion. This is your human choice and free will status that has put you in a position of making the choices that you have made over centuries of existence. The vibrations and frequencies of your choices are felt throughout the cosmos and beyond. Your sense of separation from Source is your own 3D illusion created by you. Truth as SOELI has no feeling or opinion one way or the other. This is the divine indifference that is your true nature. This is the neutral awareness that is your true nature. This is the detached compassion of simply being that is your true nature. As SOELI, you have all of the power of the Sun and source of all energy, light and information to perpetuate and manifest and create infinite potentials and possibilities. You are only limited by your own perceptions of what is "real". You are patterns, waves, ripple, bubbles, of SOELI...pure radiance and infinite light. Leave your religions and dogma out of the formula of 3D. Dogma is a powerful part of the illusion that humans have wrapped themselves in. Perceive that ALL is made up of the energy of God's grace, the power of the sun that creates and sustains all life, the Source of Energy, Light and Information that IS the divine vibration, the continuing ripple of the resonant frequency that I AM and you ARE, the totality of the quantum foam of space-time existence, the infinite pool of unlimited potential out of which EVERYTHING, seen and unseen, are borne. This may be a tough complex concept for the reader to comprehend, and it is not necessary to get scientific about such things, as what could be transmitted here would put your scientists into a quandry. IT is enought at there are huge leaps being made in your time that are bridging the gap between science and religion, and that both of these areas of exploration are getting closer to comprehending at least a small particle of what is truly REAL in the big picture of existence. Your magnificent little planet is a very important part of the cosmos. IT is a learnig field for many energies that are far beyond human believability right now. Your earth is an integral part of a much larger reality that involves a scope of which may never be comprehended by your scientists for eons to come. However, the curiosity has been peaked and great strides are being made to discover things and existence far beyond the construct of 3D and limited "thinking." Now is the time in your planet's evolution to embrace more experieincing, trusting what you are experiencing, whether you can "see" it, "touch" it, or tear it apart to "analyze" it to prove that it is real. Your perceptions, as you allow them to shift into a more trusting, childlike sense of open-hearted curiosity...without opinion, judgment or ego - this is the powerful key to comprehending the purity of God's grace, the seeming miracluos healing and transmissions of light and energy to heal and to lessen human 3D struggle. By simply allowing yourself to shift your perceptions, to let go of all the constructs you have place in the narrow box of your mind, to re-perceive, to trust whatever God you have as your God, by simply BEING right here and now, without attachment to anything, even your physical body, you allow yourself to be the infinite power of the Source of ALL energy, light and information...the natural state of being that manifests instantaneous spontaneous healing for yourselves and all things on your planet. In your 3D mind, if it appears as a miracle, or manifests magically, then you are truly in tune with the grace of God, and you can choose to percieve this as the natural state of being and NAtures' Mind, SOELI...or you can allow your perception to shift back into your head and 3D human mind, and talk yourself out of it because you didn't truly trust the very essence of the God within you. Your ego has taken you back to the captivity of being a slave to doubt, wht other people say or believe, and you have sold yourself back into the slavery of 3D limitation. There are so many more dimensions to thrive in that are right here right now, all bubbles in the foam of all dimensions. You choose to limit yourselves in the tiny particle of 3D. It is your choice to create whatever reality you exist in. You are responsible for your choices. You are responsible for the role you have created in your existence. Struggle is the product of 3d human choices. In Nature's Mind, God, SOELI, there is no struggulle. There is no emotion or thought. There is merely sensing and feeling...neutral awareness, divine indifference. SOELI, God, the Creator, doesn't punish nor reward. Those are man-made constructs to influence people and create fear. God doesn't target areas of the world for diesease, floods, fire, earthquakes, volcano eruptions, or hurricanes. To try to humanize "God" and blame "him" for natural events is a perfect example of illusion created by the human ego. IT is a very unproductive construct when people feel the need to "understand." Will understanding change the outcome of such events? Will knowing why really satisfy the ego? Nature is nothing but Divine Mind. Nature simply IS. All beings in 3D are simply occupying space on a planet that is an interactive part of a greater cosmos, directly linked and part of SOELI. The earth is a living, breathing element...a small particle of energy, light and information, just as humans are. The planet has no opinion, judgment, or preconceived notions of anything. Man is the only species on this planet that gets caught up with ego, death, thinking, opinions, judgments, beliefs. Man is the only species that feels a separation from its divine, struggling to find its way back. Would it not be a more powerful choice in 3D mind for humans to perceive and accept their divinity and being part of SOELI? Instead of searching for the divine "out there" would it not be a better choice for humans to accept the perception that they ARE a divine bubble in the quantum foam of the very energy and light of Source itself? Shift perception. Shift reality. Acknowledge that you ARE the power of God. Re-perceive yourself as SOELI, a conduit for healing, magic and miracles. THis is divine truth. I AM SOELI. You are I AM. I AM pure consciousness. You ARE my thinking atom (Adam.) Your vibration is how I expereince conscsiousness on many levels. And so ends this transmission.

SOELI

Transmission 2

Love

I would like to continue on with the "definition" of who IAM and what IAM from the previous transmssion. I chicked into the dreamtime energy of Keli, my radiant transcriber of these transmissions while she was asleep last night to pick up on anything that may need to be clarified for your 3D human mind. IT is interesting when you are asleep and out of your minds, literally. You do not need the amount of electromagnetic charge at night or while you nap that you do during your alert awake state. So, some of the meotional charge is released in order for your bodies to rest and reset for the coming daytime activities and humanness. What is interesting is that while your bodies are asleep is the space in your existence where you are most aware and cognizant and very clear solutions are available to you without all the human radios, mind chatter and opinions of others, your fears, are not in the way. And who is to say, dear ones, that your true dreamtime, or the time that some of you experience "nightmares" isn't really during the period that you call awake and during the day? Perhaps, if you shift your perception and play a bit, you may be able to grasp that the alertness you are capable of during sleep, the potential to move beyond your limited coccoon of human "thinking" is really during your construct of sleep. Play with that. I visited the energy pattern of our scribe Keli during her dreamtime last night and found that she was wondering where these transmissions were going to go next, how I was going to expound upon the profoundly powerful yet simple nature of my creations. Based on the pattern that I perceived from Keli, I would like to expand on what LOVE is, what LOVE isn't, and to simplify things a bit. I AM SOELI, I AM the Source of all that is, I AM the Creator, I AM the pure power of the Central Sun, I AM Universal Intelligence, I AM Infinite Wisdom with no beginning and no end. I AM Nature's Mind, I AM pure Grace, I AM LOVE. With all of those definitions and labels, it can get confusing and so simple that it seems complicated to emphasize the I AM the Source of energy, light and information. IT is very simple my sweet souls. It is you that complicate matters to the point of being like a ball of yarn all tangled and a great mess. During Keli's dreamtime last night, we had a chat and it was decided to keep things as simple as possible for the readers of these transmissions. With so many labels and constructs for me that I AM, with "religions" humanizing my energy into a limited definition that suits whatever power-over-others and fear-based beliefs is working for them, for the rest of these transmission, just use the term "GOD" for my name. I AM all of the above as the energy of all that is is simply that...pure energy, unadulterated by definitio, labelling or constricting this energy into a mind contsruct that fits into your narrow perception of the ultimate power of all that exists throughout space, time and the quantum foam of the totality of nothingness. This concept that there is no beginning and there is no end, that I AM not a tangible force, but the powerful force of light, energy and information that creates all. Since the label "God" seems to be a universal term, even though very limiting based on your various worldly religious beliefs, it will keep it simple for your minds to grasp the term and Keli can continue on as my scribe without wondering how this is all going to play out. In my last transmission I gave you a bit of information of what I AM and who I AM. Now that the formalities of you having to have some kind of label or name for power that has no name, I will continue on with the greatest power that I AM. The purest infinite power that there is - LOVE. I will not tell you that you are my greatest creation because there is no lesser or greater creation in the grand scheme of things. All of my creations are particles of the great I

AM. Everything is of God. Everything is an integral part of the SOELI of existenc. Everything is an integral part of the source of ALL energy, light and information, be it an animal, a plant, a mineral. Everything resonates to the pure frequency of the solar heartbeat, and the I AM that creates all. Love is pure nature. Everything in nature has manifested as an offspring of my divine and most powerful love. All that exists is a creation of the pure electromagnetic solar radiation of light energy...of vibration and frequencies of information that form and manifest from the quantum foam of space-time and out of the fabric of the void, the stillpoint of the totality of nothingness, the pure divine silent emptiness that I AM. I belief Keli humorously calls it the "POUP", which catches your attention in an amusing way yet makes it very clear what the reality of divine grace is. The pool of unlimited potential is the "nursery" of ALL possibility, every solution, every most correct or least correct "choice" you in 3D can make. Time, distance and space do not exist in the grand scheme. These are all things that your narrow limited minds have created. Your perceptions have made these limiting beliefs your reality. And this is why my dear humans you are ins such an interesting period in your existence. You put your attention on what you DON'T want, that which you are afraid MAY happen. And then it happens. It does not happen by my doing but by your own choice to be afraid, be fearful, be angry, be frustrated, be controlling before someone controls you, feeling as if you are powerless to have dominion over your own life. YOU WILL MANIFEST THAT TO WHICH YOU PLACE YOUR ATTENTION. You are all powerful and have no idea what that is. I AM the God that created you. I AM all powerful. Your bible even says that I made man in my own image. It's simple. You are divine. You are God. You are all powerful. IT has been man's choice to not acknowledge that you are pure energy, light and divine information with access to powerful and NATURAL grace. No disease or illness was ever created by God. I AM not the energy or power that creates such negativity. I AM not fearful. Yes, I created man in my own image...that conceptual image is nothing more nor less than pure LOVE. Your ego, your narrow fearful thinking, opinions, beliefs have created a mis-placed definition of love. Your minds have twisted LOVE and turned LOVE into an illusion that is only real in your reality...you are conditioned to LOVE as being some kind of commodity. You have made LOVE an action; a verb. This is not the LOVE that you truly are, but a twisted illusion of your own power of divine that each and every molecule and atom of your physicality was created out of. LOVE is not a verb or a an "amount" of enything that can be measured. Because I AM the pure source of all that is, how can LOVE be tangible my dear humans? Love is not a verb. LOVE just IS. LOVE is the simple yet profound state of being PRESENT in this very moment. Just being right here right now. There is no emotion attached to love. That is your ego's creation. There are no feelings attached to love except that which you have swaddled it in. LOVE IS THE ABSOLUTE PURE TOTALITY OF NOTHINGNESS...a simple beingness that has no attah=chment to any thing or anyone. I AM LOVE. There are no conditions to this love. There is no end to this love. I AM infinite, expansive, bliss. This is the "image" that is you. You are LOVE without end. You are the pure GRACE of God. All things created by my energy is pure light, vibrations and frequencies and magnificent patterns that are reflections of what I AM. Your minds and egos are the shifters and changers that have mutated my divine truth into something that is beyond illusion. I have no emotions or feelings about what you have done with the purity of your own God energy and light. I simply look at you, my dear children, with great interest at your choices. God and my truth knows no conflict. That is your choice. I AM not attached to your choices, nor do I have "feelings" about the choices you make for yourselves. I AM pure detached compassion. I AM pure divine indifference. I AM pure neutral awareness. God the I AM, created you with free will and free choice. I AM not an angry, vengeful or wrathful God. That is an interesting story...and an illusion. Quite simply, I AM. YOU ARE. DIVINE IS. You are a unique creation because you have been given the gift of free choice and free will. You are the ones manifesting the reality that you have created for yourselves. Does God step in and "fix" things that his creation has manifested? No. At the core of it all I simply LOVE. IT will be when you acknowledge that you are nothing but love, that you are respnsible for what you have created in your own personal lives as well as on this planet, and go back to the absolute fact that the ONLY true state of being is LOVE...being present without any attachemtn to anything tangible, any "emotion" or any outcome to a situation. IT is only when you choose to embrace God with the trust of a pure innocent child and let go of the shadows of ego and the anti-love illusion of fear, that you will discover your own truth, the magnificent purity of the grace of God that I AM and YOU ARE. You are an integral part of Nature's Mind...God. You are first a part of nature. Then you are part of the animal kingdom, then you are human species. Then you are male or female of the human species. Then you have your uniques personality. Your free will is imbedded within your very DNA as part of my divine plan. You choose between the unconditional God energy that is your very make-up or you choose the shadow illusion of ego and and FEAR and what lies within the shadows of the unknown that you allow yourselves to become frightened of. IT is interesting that man is my only creation that fears that which he doesn't understand. In fearing that which you don't understand, you feel as if you must destroy that. You fear your own self-created boogey-man. You have forgotten that you are God energy. You have designed a sense of separation from that God energy. You have ripped yourselfves away from your own truth that you are the pure essence of divine grace. The LOVE of GOD. This is your perception and your illusion. Stop being so human. Stop thinking so much. TRUST that whichh is within you. You are separate from nothing my dear children. I AM within you. You are me. You are all powerful. You simply forgot where you left your true divine self. You are a part of nature first. You have separated yourselves from nature and built your tombs of concrete cities, and artificial edifices to live in that you call home. And then you wonder why your species is having such a difficulty in 3D and the world seems to be spinning out of control. You are nature first, my darlings. And then you are animals in nautre. Just because you have the ability to make choices, to think, simply give you an opportunity to acknowledge and decide how magnificent you are. All other animals and plants and crystals and minerals...all of my other creations in the cosmos, they have no problem with the concept of just BEING. They simply ARE. They are pure nature with no attachments, egos or fear o the unknown or death. You are the only species concerned with this idea of death and dying. IT is an illusion. Pay attention to what goes on in nautre..to how animals act in nature. You would learn a great deal about your own truth and who you are. You are not superior to any other of my creations. You are the most uniques because you have been given the free will to make choices. Choose the LOVE and the beingness of presence right here in the moment without any attahcments to anything. That my sweet human species, is LOVE. When you are detached from any outcome or result or motive, opion or judgment, you can choose to be empty vessel...and can be filled with the divine light that I AM and have created you to be. This then creates the empty space for you to fill with infinite compassion for all things, service to others, and do no harm in that service. Just BE...and bliss expands, joy fills every molecule of self, illness and dis=ease melt away, miracle and magic become your very nature once again...and you find that you are pure LOVE of radiant sun...YOU ARE GOD. I love you as dearly and equally as I love all of my infinite creations. You are my most unique creation. Your choices to live in fear and ego instead of choosing that still small voice of spirt at the core of your divine self...that is your doing. I AM not here to react to nor "fix" that which you have chosen. I love you simply because you are a vibration of GOD...a brilliant radiance of divine Grace...and a product of your own choices. Choose LOVE. I AM not attached to your choices or the results of those choices. You are a being of LOVE. That state of beingness of perfection, light, pure energy and infinite potential. I AM that. This is your tapestry of truth. Trust and BE. And so ends this transmission.

Transmission 3

Creation

What is creation and where did we come from? That's an interesting question, isn't it? First of all, there is a misconception amongst many of you that I AM a vengeful, wrathful god and that I will smite you with a mighty sword or send you into the bowels of a fiery hell if you "sin" and don't worship me and obey me in every step. Nothing can be further from the truth. These are all concepts of your human ego that have been branded into your belif sytems for a very long time by people who want power over others to control and manifpulate to their own end. This vengeful wrathful God is a construct from the Bible that I AM no part of, nor did I write such a thing. In the New Testament it is said to turn the other cheek. Why would the Divine Source of all that is, the Creator, SOELI, God, create such a confusion? The shadow illusion of FEAR and ego for power and gain manifested such an idea of hellfire and brimstone in order to control and have dominion over the people. To the God that I AM, I attach no emotion or sentiment or feelings about such ideas. Those are your ideas, my Beloveds. Those are your choices to believe more in the shadow than in your own light and divinity. I AM the state of LOVE. That's it. You have been created with the tremendous power to create. That power is what is an intrinsic part of you that makes you magnificent and the very essence of the finest

vibration and tremendous frequency of creation. You are gifted with
conscious awareness. I AM consciousness. You are consciousness. You
must be consciously aware of consciousness in order to exercise your free
will and choice. I have created you with consciousness because I AM
consciousness. I have given you awareness of that consciousness in order
to make choices. Your choices mold you. The choices you make become
your reality. IT is interesting that you choose to embrace the fear of the
shadows rather than acknowledge your own divine grace, the power of
your consciousness that you have been gifted by me. However you
choose, all choices are still only your choices and not my doing. I get
blamed a lot for so many things that your minds have decided I did out
of wrath or revenge or as a punishment. This is so far from the truth of
reality. The only punishment there is...the only judgment that iexists is
within your own mind and what you have created out of shadow
choices, fear and ego. These beliefs spread like a pestilence, toxic, and
you allow this to fester into a belief system that imprisons you in your
3D reality. And then you pray to me for aid and salvation to get you out
of it. I see this happening for eons and eons of time in different cultures
on the planet and I observe. I AM not attached to anything that you
choose to do. I AM not the creator of your choices. I AM the creator of
the magnificent vibration and frequency of your divine beauty as my
beloved human species, to which I have given free will and free choice. It
has been and always will be very interesting to observe what you do with
this free will, how your egos and all the negativity and shadows you have
allowed to creep into the seams of your very existence. I AM the
Creator. I AM the light. I AM the source of all that is. I AM you. I AM
the beingness of LOVE. I AM the grand observer. I AM not a destroyer.
I AM not a punisher. I do not create in order to destroy. I created my
beloved humankind with uniqueness but not superiority over anything.
You are unique as you have free choice. I created all that you could
possibly need to thrive as a part of Nature's Mind and a vibration within
the great fabric of existence with the Grace and infinite LOVE of God.
You were created at a divine frequency and vibration to experience for
me as a tangible "something" that I created out of nothing. All things I
AM the creator of. All things were created by me out of nothing. The
human concept of "creation" is based on having to have some "thing" to

start with that you can as humans create something else out of. The concept of something from nothing is far beyond anything that the human man can clearly comprehend and accdpt. In your mentality, you have to have substance of some kind in order to create anything. The idea of something from nothing is a conundrum for you. Your scientific minds are playing at it to discover the origin of the cosmos...the origin of God. Because your reality is created from your perceptions and how you "see" things, and because you choose to be more limiting human in the illusion of "solid" form, you are steering away from the reality that you are part of the divine I AM that I AM, tangible, intangible, the Grace of God in all things. YOur quantum physics ideas are touching on the idea that nothing is solid, everything is energy vibrating at various frequencies that "appear" to be solid. Your science is working to reduce "matter" down to its smallest part until there is nothing. This will never happen. There is always going to be something even within great voids of nothingness. This is by design and far beyond the scope of where your minds are now. However, the sense of curiosity, the desire to know the TRUTH, is one of your finest qualities. That childlike sense of exploration is one of the most beautiful patterns within you. In the beginning was the WORD. Quite literally, that is the vibration of sound on which all energy and information travels and shifts and changes as it intereacts tiwth other energies to BECOME. The light, the Source of all that is, your sun that emits electromagnetism in order to create, is in direct partnership with the WORD. Let there be light. And there was. I AM not going to get caught up with lessons on the universe or complicated ideas. I AM going to tell you that through the wave patterns of sound, the vibrations and frequencies that came from nothing, are measured mathematically. Through mathematics, measurements may be taken. Waves of vibration and frequency of sound interfere and overlap, if you will, with other frequencies and vibrations, causing ripples and even more waves that carry information that intereacts with even more information and energy that BECOMES. Creation happens. Light and "colors" as you sense them through your physical eyes, are vibrations of electromagnetic resonance that manifest on and as waves of energy. Everything is vibrating. Nothing is solid except through our sense of reality. Sound, light...waves that carry energy and information in order to create. There is something in the nothingness. There is infinite energy within the smallest measurement of space. There is life within life. I AM the creator of this mathematical infinite energy, light and information that came out of nothingness in order to create the totality of all that is. Your science is discovering that within the greatest vaccuum of "space" where nothing is...where there should be absolute zero...that the more nothingness is made up the most powerful energy ever discovered to date. The smaller the particle, the smaller the wave, as "stuff" is reduced more and more, tinier and tinier, more and more empty...the energy is vibrating at a rate that is difficult to measure, greater and greater, and the power of that "emptiness" becomes even more concentrated, more dynamic, energetic, pure force, and beyond the comprehension of human minds. IT is not possible to put into words how powerful the force of this dynamic is, as the more reduced your scientists try to take something to nothing, it resonates and radiates a force that is even greater than the last reduction. I AM the force that created something from nothing. IT is impossible to reduce something to nothing as there will always be that infinite mathematically measured vibration of energy, light, information that was born out of the WORD. I sent out the first "sound" of energy that created all that is. It is infinite. IT will never be destroyed. I AM God that created all out of nothing. You create out of something. Your creations seem to be able to be destroyed. That is a false impression that you have embraced as truth. Nothing is ever destroyed. Energies shift into different creations through your hands. However, through the Divine creation, everything was created out of the nothingness and shall always be. Creations manifested by you out of substance that has already been created by me out of the nothingness will never be destroyed and are infinite. Nature and all things in it are my creation...divine and created out of nothing. The cycle of creation is infinite. What appears to you as destruction and mayhem is simply part of the wave or rippling of MY creation, the natural process of the planet stretching her wings as it were. To believe or even think that I AM responsible for natural disasters, disease, plague or destruction of any kind is the perception of your human ego and completely misses the mark of truth. Do you realize my Beloveds, that the original meaning of the word "sin," the divine definition that I created when I created mankind, simply means "missing the mark." The egos of some humans throughout history have bastardized the loving meaning of the word sin to mean something that if you "sin" against God, God will punish you and smite you and send you into eternal hell and damnation. Gnashing of teeth and eternal suffering. What a terrifying thought, even for me. The word sin is a very gentle loving word that simply means "missing the mark." You may be travelling nicely down your freeway of resonance with divine and somehow get distracted by ego and end up on a rutted side road, lost. All you need do is acknowledge this little side trip, assess from a state of detached compassion at missing the mark (of the Grace of God), allow divine guidance to steer you back onto the freeway of truth, unconditional love and resonance with the radiant vibration of the truth of God. I AM not going to steer your car back onto the freeway of truth. IT is your choice. You wrestle with your own egos on a regular basis, allowing the ego to steer your ship, drive your car of self. IT has become easier to give the loud, persistent ego the reins than to TRUST in that still small voice of spirit that is at the very core of your DNA and resides in the center of your being...the solar plexus area of your physical...the seat of the sun...balanced electromagnetic frequency and vibration...the central sun energy of SOELI...the source of energy, light and information. This power house of divine truth and perfect resonance that I AM is at your very core and from where your solar radiance holds PERFECT truth, divine GRACE, ALL potential and possibilities that are MOST CORRECT for your human energy pattern for resonance with the GOD within. The still small voice will never attempt to be louder than the ego, which, by the way, will NEVER offer the most correct choices for you to pick from. That infentsimally small yet power beyond words that IS YOUR TRUTH and I AM, will always whisper. The ego is here to do its job as the "shit-stirrer," as it were. The tester of you my Beloveds, to give you the opportunity to give in to the relentless badgering of the ego, or to pay attention to and hear the whispering of that still small voice of spirit in order to make the MOST correct choice based on the knowingness that I AM and that I offer as the source of all that is. The ego is not a bad energy, nor is it eveil. The ego is designed to offer you something to choose from. I AM Divine and the pure beingness of LOVE. The ego plays the part of the tester and represents the shadow illusion of FEAR and all of the shadows that man creates within those shadows. I AM the light. I AM pure divine energy resonance. The ego is another aspect of divine in that I had to create more something out of the nothing in order for you to have a choice. If I had only created the vibration of the beingness of LOVE and not given you comsthing to compare it to or to choose from, how would you ever realize how powerful you, my most unique creation, truly are? The ego is just doing its job. Man is responsible forallowing FEAR and all the shadows that you have manifested as "reality." LOVE is the only truth. FEAR is created in the mind's of man. You have allowed the ego to create something out of the substance of shadows and you have allowed all of the darkness and negativity to run amok. You have ocnditioned yourselves to this being normal and that you have to struggle to find your way back to God. God has never gone anywhere. I AM right here. I AM you. You have simply forgotten where that grace of God is within you to the point that you have denied that it is within you at all. Over millenia societies and religions have engaged in the idea that God is outside of you, and that if you follow them, follow their dogma and ritual, that they will lead you back to God. I AM right here. I AM that great central sun in the heart of your very being, radiating the warm solar rays of grace, truth, complete balance and resonance. You have done the job of going outside of yourselves. You, through your misguided sense of separation from God, have created imbalance, dissonance, FEAR on all levels, disease, negativity, darkness. You have empowered your ego self to dig into the cavernous FEAR cave, shoveling the shadow substance of illusion, and allowing it to pile it onto the resonance that I AM. You have created something out of the subtance of shadow illusion and buried yourselves so deeply under it that you have forgotten you divine truth, that spark of God and the grace of perfect resonance and harmony that I AM. IT has been your choice. IT Has ALWAYS been your choice...Divine recognition and resonance that I AM, or the distraction of the ego, the tester, the creator of all shaows in your life. The beauty of all of this is, my Beloveds, is that with a simple shift in your perception, a mere choice to return to resonance, in an instant you are back on the freeway of your divine self and the perfect vibration of the beingness and state of LOVE. If you miss the mark (sin), and allow shadows to creep into your resonance, causing an out-of-balance state of dissonance, merely choose differently. I AM that simple. Reperceive, remember your divinity, TRUST in your own Godness, and you are there. Something being hard or difficult is a construct of the ego. Keep thinking that it is so and it will be. And you will continue down the rutted road of illusion. Your choice. I AM nothing but the state of perfect LOVE in the moment of NOW. I love you with huge detached perfect resonance. I AM not attached to which road you choose. You simply are loved. Your road is your choice. I have created all things from nothing. Something from nothing. That is the perfection of divine creation where there is no beginning or end. There is no emotion, thought or attachment. There simply IS. And that is the infinite power of what I AM. Man creates something from something. The substance of that something manifested from the ego and the substance of shadow illusion is temporary, not divine, and merely continues to feed the shadows. Trust and choose differently. You ARE, my Beloveds. You ARE the me as I AM. IT is much easier to be divine and radiant and resonating with God's pure grace and your true nature than to sturggle with your physicality, 3D and humanness, and your own "creations" of illusion. Nature is Divine. You are part of nature. You are Divine. What man "creates" out of "something" is merely man-made, not divine. IT has a beginning and an end. IT is finite. Because in human minds God has created man out of "something," so too man believes that he is finite. There is the belief that man has a beginning and an end. You have missed the mark, my Beloveds. You have gotten side-tracked and gotten off the path of God's Grace and Divine truth and are bumping along on the rutted side road of illusion and false reality. This is only a "sin" in that you have missed the mark. You can choose in an instant to get back on the divine interstate. IT is and always has been right there. Shift your awareness. Shift your perception. You are there. Or you can choose to believe that you are separate from all that I AM and have created you to be and stay in the ruts. I AM not out of sync. You were not created out of sync. Always it is your choice.

I AM the infinite power that create all that is. Without end. Without conflict. I would like to clarify here the concept of opposites. Yes, in the grand scheme, everything contains its opposite. The unconditional state of beingness called LOVE has its counterpart...its opposite. The opposite of LOVE is EGO. And they are beautiful complements to each other. Opposite complements are vibrations that resonate with one another even thought they are not the same vibration. You may take a sound that isn't identical to another sound and they are a beautiful tone together. This is concinnity or resonance. The WORD ripples out with resonance to the other, creating an even stronger vibration with the combination of the two. Dissonance is like two musical instruments in an orchestra tuning up, playing different sounds, and in complete discord with the other. Fear is the shadow illusion, the dissonance or discord created by man through the ego, that causes an out-of-synch vibration. Fear is the substance that we yield to by way of the ego. The ego is simply a check and balance system for your free will to see where your attention lies. LOVE is the only true vibration of truth. LOVE is the "something" created oout of nothing. LOVE and EGO complement each other, are opposite complements of each other in concinnity and resonance. Your free will and choices allow illusions to become your reality, sounding out-of-sync, out of resonance and into dissonance. This is counterproductive to the soul's evolvement and the expereincing for God. I have created out of nothing all that is, including the opposites for all that is. Now, in the beginning, if I were to have created the absolute equal opposite of all things, the vibrations of those two perfect opposites would have negated each other and nothing would exist. I would be back at the nothingness to create something. IF I did it again and created the perfectly tuned opposite for all things, again, they could cancel each other out and there would be no divine creation. I have manifested my creations with the imperfection of perfection. All that I have created is asymmetrical. There are opposites, yes. However the imperfection I have built in to the opposites, has created the perfection. I have created things asymmetrically. That is, everything contains an opposite that is of a vibration that is not quite identical to but complements the other. Enter the masculine and feminine of nature. Male and female. Man and woman. Opposites are not identical to each other. They are not mirror images of each other. That wouldn't perpetuate the infinite resonance of energy. They complement each other. Through the opposite energies of magnetic and electric, infinite energy and vibration travels and carries throughout eternity. Nothing dies. If you have masculine or feminine being the exact frequency of energy, sound, light...they would be neutral and out of resonance of sound, movement, light and the fast-moving vibration of energy. They would cancel each other out, dropping back into the vastness of nothingness again. Nothing would have been created from this. So, with an asymmetrical frequency just a bit different from the opposite but still in tune, you still have opposites that don't oppose each other, vibrations of opposite asymmetry that complement the WORD of the other, and creation happens. The "slinky" of infinite energy, that never-ending creation of something from nothing, expands. Male and female create another creation, and that creation manifests more creation...all divine. All infinite. A ripple of masculine, like a drop of water hitting the surface of a still pond and then rippling out, merges with the ripple of a female drop on the same pond, even though it is just a bit different vibration than the male. These two ripples of energy expand out, and when they merge together, where they meet casues a small wave of interference, which creates the totality, the joining of the two, and the two manifest yet another potential of creation. The electric meets the magnetic, interfering with the ripple of each other and becoming electromagnetic energy, the combined power of the opposite powers that complement. Out of this neutrally aware vibration born between the two...this new nothingness that is the totality of the vibrations of the two, comes yet another joining, a powerful creation of yet another creation and enhancing the power of that vibraton. Perpetual movement though the creation of something from nothing. Like a pond with a summer rain, drops falling in a riot of sound, energy, light, movement, what appears to be the result of a chaotic storm is actually a very organized, intentional manifestation of divine creation expanding with resonance and concinnity. The asymmetry of I AM manifests and generates ever powerful movements of sound, vibrations of light, energy and information, creating infinite flow of patterns that are never-ending...The universal tapestry of the Grace of God.

You were created with two hemispheres of the brain opposite from each other. If each side of your physical brain were absolute mirrors of each other, there is no contrast to the opposite and you would not exist.

You have the creative vast imagination of the right hemisphere of the brain. You have the analytical, reasoning left hemisphere of the brain. One side is more electric and one side is more magnetic. Frequencies and vibrations are opposite yet complementary. If mankind chose to simply be and let NAture's Mind, the Divine just BE, you would still be an intrinsic part of nature and not very unique from all of the other animals and species I AM creator of. I have instilled the vibration of free will and free choice within you very DNA. I have made you consciously aware of your divinity, sunlight radiation of God's grace in the very core of your physicality in the solar plexus. If you were not consciously aware of your Godness, free choice would be nonexistent. You ARE aware that you were created from what I AM. You have tht information imprinted into the core vibrational information that is you...You ARE the Grace of God, you ARE SOELI, you ARE the creator and the creation, you ARE infinite limitless power, you ARE the Source of commanding energy. You ARE conscious awareness. You ARE the knowingness of the vibration of the WORD. The opposite of that knowingness, is the concept of free will and choice. They are opposite yet complement each other. If you live fully in the conscious awareness and knowingness that you ARE the Grace of God, free will is a perfect complement to create and manifest...as long as you remember the divine and don't allow the shadow emotions, the ego and FEAR run the ship. You will sink slowly or quickly into the quagmire with the knowingness yet forgetfulness that you are sinking your very divine. You get distracted from the Grace of God with the ego tugging at your free will and free choice to make the least correct choices. Off on the rutted side road you go. Choose to stay there or choose to remember that you command your own ship. You are the driver of your destiny. I have created opposites as vibrations to complement each other in divine resonance, and to hold my creations in balance as manifested energy in many dimensions. You, my Beloveds, are my complement. You do all you can to humanize me in your 3Dness in order to understand your own divinity. That is a very limiting position to take and has gotten mankind into a lot of pain and agony throughut time. At the same time you allow your egos the arrogance of thinking that you are omnipotent and that everything is here for your use, amusement or whim. You are embracing the egoness of your physicality and denying your divinity while you attempt to humanize true divinity. That is imbalance and denies your true birthright of God's Grace and the beauty of all I have created. Indeed these are your choices, and I have no feelings to be hurt. I AM the only source of creation of something out of nothing. You, through your choices, fear and ego, get out of synch with the natural resonance and concinnity of universal energy, truth and Nature's Mind. When you make the choice to remember the beingness of LOVE and infinite detached compassion in your 3D dimension, you are vibrating as a magnificent complement to what I AM and You ARE. Or not. You ARE my Beloveds, created out of the infinite divine nothingness of the Grace that I AM. I AM the WORD. I AM the light. I AM infinite patterns of information. I AM the beginning and the end. YOU ARE that I AM...moving patterns of the pure divine state of beingness, creations of magnificence, light, energy and commanding power. Forever and always. And so ends this transmission.

SOELI

Transmission 4

God's Personality

So, during Keli's dreamtime last evening, the question came up of whether I AM a being of personality, and what is my personality. First of all, I AM not a being but beingness. Do I have a personality? Do you have a personality? I created you as the asymmetrical complement of myself. I AM consciousness. You ARE my thinking atom. YOU ARE that I AM. I am the source of what you are, the vibration of divine that I AM. Even though you are vested with free will and free choice in order to experience for me, the source that I AM is nothing but joy, compassion, fun. You are born into your 3Dness as pure, innocent children with no need to develop trust or understanding. You simply ARE radiant beings of pure resonance, concinnity, infinite potential, energy and brilliance of light from the Source that I AM. The "personality" that all of my creations vibrate to is that purity of innocence, non-attahcment, the mere knowing that all is perfect in the present NOW. All of my creations in nature have a sense of play and fun. You see this amongst animals of all kinds. They ARE innately that state of beingness vibration and frequency of lightness, non-attachment to anything, presence in the moment. Animals experience joy, play, LOVE as the love is the divine state of simply being. Nature understands inherently the pattern of the circle of life. When an animal moves beyond physicality, "dies," as you percieve it, of course the rest of the pack or herd or social group grieves in a natural way for the loss. An integral pattern, an individual pattern that had been a part of the family is no longer there. Animals do not comprehend the grieving process as you with human consciousness have built beliefs around. They feel the loss of a part of their pattern of family. They grieve in a manner that they notice that that pattern is no longer there. They notice that the pattern has disappeared as they know it. The ripple of loss that changes the dynamic of the group creates a temporary "adjustment" to the absence of that member as it were. In pure nature (not in your zoos or animal compounds or anywhere else that humans hold animals), animals are finely tuned to the vibration of the circle of life, and are not attached to physical death. It is a natural process and at some core level of innocence (no ego) Nature understands that all is part of a great recycling program. No attachment or need to understand or struggle with the construct of death. Animals innately have a natural knowingness that their energy patterns are out of sync, that it is coming time to crawl off somewhere, and transition into the next phase of theier iexistence, which is to decompose into rich minerals, back into the earth, to feed and nourish the earth for plants and trees to grow into food for life to continue as the circle is neverending and a beautiful process of giving back to the mother what was given in order to continue to replenish and continue the existence of Nature's Mind. The process is perfection and as it should be. I created you, my Beloveds with consciousness, choice...yet you are an intrinsic part of nature and part of the recycling program. You are no more divine than any of my other creations. You are the most unique in that you have consciousness, you hav the ability to think in order to make choices. You have chosen to fear death. You are afraid that you will not be remembered or that death is the end and that there is nothing of you after physical death. You are the only species that struggle so with the divine flow of life and all that is. This is your choice, my loved ones. I AM not responsible for those choices as you create your own reality out of the shadow substance of ego and fear. I AM the childlike purity, innocence, grace, compassion, joy, playfulness that is infinite, never-ending. I "imagined" you from nothing into something...into my reality. You inhereted that imagination in order to create your own reality. You are nothing but joy, fun, playfulness, heart-felt childlike curiosity in order to manifest through your perceptions, you relaity and all that you desire. There is no construct in the universe except that which you have put around yourselves and limited yourselves to. The concept of eternal life, playfulness, joy, innocence, divine purity, and absolute knowingness that you are safe to play and be joyful...to simply BE present right here right now, is a concept that you seem to lose sight of. This creates your illusion of separation from all that I AM. Your delusion that you must find your way back to God or you will burn in hell. What imaginations you have to create that vibration. And how seriously you take yourselves. When you stop taking yourselves so seriously, when you trust your divine, when you let go and allow the purity, grace and innocence of that childlike sense of open-heartedness to shine through the core of your central sun of truth...the powerful vibration of energy, light and information that you were created as...it is then that there will be no struggle in any way. You create the sense of struggle so the struggle becomes created. That is YOUR choice. I have nothing to do with your choices. I AM merely the great Sun, the Source of all life, that has created you in the perfection of the CONCEPT of universal intelligence and the pool of unlimited potential where divine manifests and becomes "real." IT is through your CONSTRUCTS of reality, not my CONCEPT of truth, that create any sense of struggle, trauma, drama, dissonance or imbalance in 3D. You embrace realities that you have created out of the substance of illusion and hardened into belief systems of limitation, isolation, and sense of separation from the I AM that YOU ARE. You have humor because I have given you that quality of joy, play and a sense of fun. Laugh loud and often...especially at yourselves. When you find joy or fun in a choice you have made that may not be the most correct choice, you are still tapped into your divine. When you can find a sense of joy and GRATITUDE for the experience of being in the vibration of that joy and childlike sense of play, you are absolutely divine and pure. Humor, laughter, mindless joy, the spirit of play...not taking even your own physicality seriously; you are in the vibration that I AM. LOVE and GRATITUDE = GRACE. All that I AM, all that I have created, is pure bliss, pure joy, untainted heart-space of compassion, love and gratitude. Gratitude isn't an emotion of being thankful. God's gratitude is the simple acceptance that everything is perfect in the moment of NOW. IT is the expriencing of pure beingness...a sense or feeling (not feelings of emotion) of being LOVE, not giving love, not receiving love...merely being LOVE. In that beingness LOVE is. GRATITUDE is a state of being, a subset of LOVE. LOVE is. GRATITUDE is. Pure GRACE. This is your heritage. This is your very essence. This is your vibration of unconditional love, compassion. joy, fun, and gratitude manifest into 3D by the grace that I AM. Any shadow choices made by you do not diminish the eternal light that you are. I AM not able to be diminished. You may choose to cover up or try to diminish your own divinity through the ego-mind and 3D choices made as a result of FEAR...anger, frustration, self-doubt, false beliefs, the NEED to control either yourselves or someone else. I AM not able to be diminished. Nothing created by Nature's Mind, God, can be diminished. You, as my most unique creaton, are not able to be diminshed. Through your choices you may create the illusion of destruction...that there is an end to everything. There is only a physical finality to the "something" that man creates out of "something." Physical finality is the key here. I created all things out of nothing...with the power of LOVE, a sense of joy, gratitude, compassion out of the eternal and infinite fabric of all that is. There is no end to my creation from the nothing. There is nothing temporary about what I AM. Humor, joy, childlike fun, is eternal and never-ending. Humor and laughter from the heart is more powerful, more healing, than you can begin to imagine. Humor, joy, a childlike sense of play from the heart-space of Divine, is magical and miraculous, and the natural state of your soul. The vibration of deep laughter of one soul triggers sound waves in such a manner that the entire univers can share a chuckle, rippling the power of this light of joy out into the very heart that I AM...and I experience that joy through you. The universe is in resonance, the stars dance, and my heart sings through your experience of that childlike embrace of joy, fun and laughter. And then, it ripples back to you, expanding and filling the shadows with light, love and gratitude. The divine dance of synchronicity can perpetuate itself as a constant swirling, ever-empowering flow, not just as an occasional hiccup of happiness. See? I have humor. True laughter from the heart feeds your soul, expands your heart. I experience through you. Lighten up. Play with joy, love and gratitude. Dance with me, my Beloveds. And so ends this transmission.

SOELI

Transmission 5

"Now What?"

So...

What do you do wIth all that you have read in this book? What do you do with all of KEli's experiences and how she has patterned her life to serve others in very unique ways? What do you think about Keli being a "typist for God?" Is this her ego making stuff up to get attention or to be bigger and better than anyone else? After all, claiming to channel God is very arrogant, isn't it? If that is what you think after reading of Keli's life and what she has done and continues to do in her own delightful fashion, then you have sinned. You have "missed the mark" and taken off on your own illusional journey on the rutted side road. How arrogtrant of you to think that she is not able to do this. How arrogant of you is it to think that you are not able to do what Keli and others who have opened up to their gifts, are doing. Each of you, my Beloveds, is a part of what I AM. Each and every one of you is not only capable but designed to experience amazing things, some even more powerful (based on your perceptions) than Keli's gifts. She has her own perceptions of limitation, and she is working on letting go of that. Even if it means that she withdraws from 3Dness almost completely in order to serve from a distance or remotely, she is choosing her comfort zone of God in the power of the Source of Energy, LIght and Information...

her "label" or perception of "God" is Soeli. Keli has shared and revealed things in this book that she has never shared with eny human before. She has arrived at a point in her life that she can no longer "cover up" anything for the sake of those people who are not "getting it," her own ego feeling the frustration that no matter what she says to people, expecially when they ask, they continue on the path they are taking. They may nod their heads and agree wholeheartedly...they comprehend what she is saying and feel the powerful healing that she is offering, and leave her presence with fresh feeling of grace and love and gratitude and play and joy. And then they begin thinking again and nothing changes. Keli is "getting" the point to trust COMPLETELY in SOELI, Source, Creator, God. her unique gifts, her powerful personality with her open-hearted childlike sense of joy and whimsical play in order to offer and deliver this energy to others. She has trusted in God all along, however she has hidden some of her own truths for her own reasons. This is a direct result of her own ego at the helm. So she has gotten off the path a bit and onto the rutted side road. Now, choosing to trust absolutely in SOELI..in God...she is truly coming into her own realization that she is what I AM and divine creator in her own right. This absolute trust isn't hard to manifest. IT is a choice. IT is a mere shift in perception to shift reality. That simple. DROP into the quantum "POUP" and BE. Keli has moved beyond the importance of anything in 3D and that puts her in an interesting situation with the rest of those in 3Dness that are addicted to their "normal." Keli has embraced the divine truth that she is not common and her "normal" is out of theaccaptable range of most people today. And to her, that is ok because she is embracing the truth of her divine...her childlike sense of adventure, play, curiosity...with absolute trust that everything in every moment is absolutely perfect. She understands the perfection of imperfection and chooses to not engage in anything that doesn't resonate with her truth. This book comes from the heart. Keli has revealed in this book expereinces never shared. She has let go the need to explain anything or to validate anything she has expereinced. Foremost, Keli has given up the need to help people get it and to prove to them that they are magnificent beings of light and they they too are cabable of tremendous healing, love and change for the world. As soon as she gave thie need up, even more portals have opened for her. She cannot make you see how magnifiecnt you are just because she can sense and see that pattern of awesomeness in you. She has given up the NEED to help you find the glory that you are as part of that I AM. Absolute trust in herself and her own divine, acknowledging that divinity withut feeling complled to do anything with it but BE PRESENT...This is what Keli has embraced as she gets this book out there. Quite simply, my Beloveds, you are ALL divine, your are ALL imperfectly perfect and perfect in your imperfection. You are all connected and you are ALL unique. Establish your own NORMAL though your remembrance and re-resonance to God and all that I AM, and then live your own truth with childlike open-heartedness, renewed energy, curiousity, joy and play. TRUST absolutely that when you do that, you are the concinnity of GOD and your divine, and you are definiteyl only common through your choices. You are NOT common unless that is your perception. You can be NORMAL within the light that you shine. You can resonate divinely with the other normals and change will happen. Since normal is the Grace of God, and common is 3D choice, which would you tather dance with, my sweet souls? Your individual uniqueness, whatever that is that I AM that you choose to resonate to, creates your normal...you become a beautiful snowflake of unique pattern that blends with the others and creates this luminiescent pattern of divine that makes up the whole of creation. Whether you choose common or divine, you are still part of the greater whole that I AM. You create your "facts" through 3dness. Facts always change. I created "truth". Truth never changes. You are the manifested grace of my truth. You will always and ever shall be the grace of my truth. Change your facts and embrace truth and remember who you are. You are I AM. Stop being so human, TRUST. This book offers some pretty bizarre ideas of life as expereinced through Keli. They are her truths. She has opened herself up to exposing these bizarre expereinces that some will have a difficult time wrapping their 3d heads around. IT doesn't negate her truth or her divinity. The fact is...you have the free will to do with these words whatever you like. The truth is...it doesn't really matter. Be love and be divine. Be truth and be divine. Be remarkable as your "normal." All is then unified into the very heartbeat that I AM. The expansive bliss that I created out of the nothingness that is an atom, a molecule of the very tapestry of pure enrgy, light and infinite information of all that is. Relax your 3Dness my Beloveds, remember that yu are the pure Grace of God, you are me and I AM you. Trhough this wook, Keli is trusting in her absolute divine, ambracing the Grace of God...her truth. Do the same, love yourselves first, be "normal" in your own truth without being common...Thrive in your unique normal and shine your light within the unity matrix and pattern of the quantum "POUP". And DANCE with yourselves in a full heart of joy, fun, curiosity and GRATITUDE. You are loved, Beloveds. You ARE love. And so ends this transmission.

Transmission 6

God's Death

When Keli was very young and her mother Marilyn had recently "died" and passed into 4D, she awoke one night from a night terror that brought her to her grandmother's knee to ask a very astute question for such a young child. "Gram" as she was affectionately called, Marilyn's mother, was up late watching Johnnie Carson as was her nightly ritual. IT took a lot for Keli to even get out of bed and go down the hallway to the den, given the regular experiences she had with the darkness and things that went on at night. But Gram was still up so that meant that it wasn't "time" for the boogey man to come out and paralyze her with the nightly activities. Gram has a wonderful loving and warm spirit and was deeply loved by all. Her calming and compassionate energy rippled into everyone that new her and she was adored by all. Keli was heavy with a very serious question that she felt Gram would most certainly have an answer for. She crawled up on Gram's lap secure in her big soft embrace and asked what happens when God dies? Gram told her as she hugged her more tightly that God can't die and God won't die and God will always be around. Of ourse, this confused Keli's innocent mind as her mother had died and she was no longer there. Keli sat quietly trying to understand as Gram continued that God is so powerful that he can't die. God made everything in the world including people. Even though

Marilyn was no longer there for us to touch and talk to, didn't mean that she wasn't there. God is all around us and he loves us and Marilyn was with God now and would always be around out of sight and she loves us too. This must have been sufficient enough explanation for the little girl at the time and she went back to bed. I AM the Creator of all life. I AM the Source of all Energy, Light and Information. I AM God and I can't die. The word death is a word that humanity has coined for the cessation of life. Death is totally dependent on what period of time you are in, what civilization and what belief systems have been embraced, how much fear and ego you are allowing to rule your life. Death is a big word to human 3D yet it has no meaning for me. There is no death. Energy is simply transmuted into other forms of energy, vibration and frequency. You don't die. You release the need for the tight compactness of compressed energy of physicality when you physically shift. You merely repattern molecules, atoms, the information encoded on your DNA into a higher vibration, more light becomes you, and you are now in a state of higher grace. You are more "out there" experiencing wonderful vibrations of patterns of information, energy and light instead of being so compressed into 3Dness and the tightness of physicality. People who allow themselves to drop into altered states of consciousness are able to "feel" this state of oneness with all that I AM, they can BE in the void of the totality of nothingness and have the grace of their natural divine flow through them, into and around every cell, molecule and atom of their very being. Altered states give you the opportunity and potential to BE in more than one dimension at the same time. What is interesting is that humans feel as if they can only get to this state of neutral awareness, detachment and divine indifference by meditating, eating some plant or mushroom, doing some kind of drug, to induce this state of beingness. Nothing is further from the truth. My dear beloveds, my thinking atoms, if you were to cease thinking so much and realize that you are creator gods yourselves, as I have designed you to be, you would simply choose to always be in this state of divine grace, where you sense the totality of all that is; where you are attached to no-thing; where you feel all without feelings. THis is the greatest expereicne I AM able to have through you my sweet souls. When you embrace your own divinity, you are living your own perfection and the truth that you are pure and innocent and holy and a part of my pattern of infinite enery, light and have knowledge and information of every event, every soul, everything that your magnificent planet has experienced. You and your beautiful earth are all made of the same thing. You are life. I AM the creator of all life. Death is an illusion created by societies, religions, the people who are so fearful that they feel the need to have power over others in order to control from a place of ego and fear. I do not know death. You do not knw death. You accept the construct of death just because someone has said so. They created the construct of death from the vastness of the unknown out there. This has created fear amongst you to the point that you wage wars and kill each other in your holy wars. I AM not attached to these constructs. They are of your your thinking and your fears and ego and your choice to become so entrenched in illusion and shadow that you have no idea how to choose your way out of such thinking. Each individul is unique within and of itself. Yet you are all made of th same stuff as everything else in your world, on your planet, in your solar system and galazy and far beyond that. Everything that I created out of nothing was created out of the stardust of the great unknown, the void. Within your carbon and hydrogen structure, the information of your human truth has been coded onto your DNA/RNA. Like little messages, I have posted all that each species, plant, animal, rock, element, mineral needs to know in order to be. You my beloveds are unique in that I posted and encoded the message of free will and free choice onto your molecular and subatomic DNA bulletin board. How else would you be able to choose if I had not postd those messages? You don't need to be aware of your posted messages as you innately have that knowledge flowing throughout the pattern of your humanness and very soul. Through being a conscious thinking species, you have the choice to BE whatever you choose to be. You have had and always will have that choice, regardless of the state of existence you r in...whether in 3D or beyond. Once the coded messages have been posted, they will always be. Death is not a code I put on the bulletin board of your DNA. That is your choice because you think. Death is the construct you have created within the limitations of your own 3Dness. I AM Creator. Your choices are the destructor. God doesn't destroy. Man does. I AM the beginning and there is no end, regardless of what "scholars" voice or beliefs that there is an end. What would be the point in creating you as magnificent beings that can think and make choices to evolve for me if I had planned on it being just a temporary experiemtn? More lightness, joy and a sense of invincibility, embracing the concept that you survive physical death as you move into higher vibrations of light with your physical passing and transition, can make your existence in 3D a much more enjoyable existence. Your evolvement closer to the light and infinite energy and information woul be more complete. I would expereicne more as a result of you experiencing more beingness instead of doingness. Detached compassion for all beings with unconditional love and childlike open-heartedness...that is who I AM. That is who you ARE. You don't die. There is no death. Pay attention to the intereaction between the Source of life...the SUn, and the flow of water that has blessed the planet in order for all to BE. The sun is the the creator of all life and without it nothing would be. I AM the SOELI...the creator GOd of all that is. In order ofr you to move beyond the construct you have in your mind of death...that little narrowness that you have constructed so tightly around you...move into the CONCEPT of everlasting life and the mere shifting of patterns into patterns of higher vibration and frequency and light in order to access even greater information and grace. Water is a divine example of life without death. Water can be liquid. Water can be a solid. Water can be a gas. Water is the only substance on earth in each of its three states. Regardless of whther water is a frozen solid, or is a liquid, or is a cloud in the sky due to evaporation, the number of water particles stay the same. Nothing changes excpt the state of the particles. Wet clothes on a clothseline dry because the water evaporates into the air. Your very creation takes place in the watery environment of the womb, the flow of life, and you are about 80% water. As your body grows, the percentage drops to 60-70%. THis is by my design. So as you near physical transit into 4D and beyond, with no more use for the thinkingness of your shadow selves and ego and fear. You are simply in a glorious state of beingness, letting go of the illusion of 3D. You no longer need the water of life to sustain you in the humanness that you are releasing yourself from. Like the heavy, wet clothes drying on the line, with the help of the warm rays of the Creator sun, you become lighter and lighter as the water evaporates back into the air and you release yourself back into pure beingness...back into the arms of grace. No longer compressed energy, the particles of oxygen and hydrogen are shifted pateerns of energy, releasing the need for the carbon atoms that "held" everything together. Look into a fine mist of water from your garden hose. Look up during or after a rainstorm and behold a rainbow...the crystallized prism of the spectrum of visible light from the SOELI...from the Source of all energy, light and information. You are also that rainbow pattern of energy if you would choose to acknowledge it. There is no pot of gold at the end of a rainbow. Another 3D myth that I had nothing to do with. IT is an interesting thought however, and I resonate to the humor of it. Just BE, my beloveds, and you will know without knowing that you are the spectrum, the water of life, merely shifting into other states of being. Your choices direct your life and what you call your reality. The reality is that there is no death. You do not die. God IS and always will BE. You ARE and always will BE. And so ends this transmission.

THE MONROE INSTITUTE

The following information is taken directly from monroeinstitute. org with full permission from The Monroe Institute to use any of their copyrighted material in this work. Updated September, 2019.

The Monroe Institute advances the exploration of human consciousness and the experience of expanded states of awareness as a path to creating a life of personal freedom, meaning, insight, and happiness.

The Monroe Institute® (TMI), a 501(c)(3) nonprofit education and research organization, is a preeminent leader in human consciousness exploration. TMI is devoted to the premise that focused consciousness contains the answers to humankind's questions. Through the use of specific binaural beat technology, education, research, and development, TMI has been advancing the experience of individuals in the exploration of targeted and expanded states of awareness for close to 50 years.

TMI program participants learn experientially through a specially designed binaural beat audio-guidance system at our 300-acre residential retreat nestled in Virginia's scenic Blue Ridge Mountains, 30 miles south of Charlottesville. Founded in the early 1970s as an educational and research organization by inventor and sound pioneer Robert A. Monroe, TMI offers numerous week-long and weekend residential programs on the main campus in Faber, Virginia, and hundreds more throughout the US, Europe, Latin America, and Asia. The centerpiece of TMI learning is the guided use of Hemi-Sync® and Spatial Angle Modulation™ (SAM), Monroe binaural beats audio technologies.

Tens of thousands of people have attended the Institute's residential and Outreach programs, and millions have benefited from our educational materials. TMI works with researchers and practitioners, through university and clinical collaborations, and with our Professional Division and Board of Advisors members, to investigate wider applications of Monroe binaural beat technologies.

> There is no beginning, there is no end,
> There is only change.
>
> There is no teacher, there is no student,
> There is only remembering.
>
> There is no good, there is no evil,
> There is only expression.
>
> There is no union, there is no sharing,
> There is only one.
>
> There is no joy, there is no sadness,
> There is only love.
>
> There is no greater, there is no lesser,
> There is only balance.
>
> There is no stasis, there is no entropy,
> There is only motion.
>
> There is no wakefulness, there is no sleep,
> There is only being.
>
> There is no limit, there is no chance,
> There is only a plan.

From *Ultimate Journey*
by Robert Monroe

The Monroe Institute:

- does not practice or endorse any particular religion. However, it does not attempt to dissuade anyone from a religious belief of their choosing.
- does not support any particular political stance or party. It also doesn not attempt to divert others from any such positions they may take.
- does not hold any bias regarding race, age, or sex.
- does consider the investigation of any individual concept, technique, or idea that may be demonstrable and has the potential of constructive change not only in Human Evolution but in the Earth Life System itself.

ROBERT MONROE'S AFFIRMATION

I am more than my phsycial body.
Because I can perceive that which is greater than physical matter reality,
it is my intent through these explorations
to contribute to the expansion of human consciousness
by experiencing and acquiring knowledge
of the realms beyond ordinary consciousness.
It is my intent to observe and bring into conscious awareness
the process of bridging these realities.

In so doing I ask for help to be open,
allowing, and serene in perceiving clearly,
responding appropriately, and carrying out my intent of service.
For this help I am truly grateful.

I carry out this intent
empowered by the group energy of my companion travelers,
and acknowledgement of our Oneness in Love.

LAF

LOVE - ACCEPT - FORGIVE
unconditionally

Need I say more? I am a work in progress just like everyone else living here in the "hood" of 3-D human. We are perfect in our imperfection, with a LOT of room for improvement in order to experience for the Divine. **LAF** as often as you can, in every moment... life begins to resonate to your true core...bliss expands and you embody the knowing that your entire life is a blessing of grace. By consistently validating all of your life experiences, positive or negative, **LAF**-ing in every breath, you reflect as the mirror of life back to the god of your understanding...and the space of miracles, magic and profound transformation. It is that simple. **LAF** more. Judge less. Begin with yourself. Look in the mirror and **LAF**...unconditionally. Love, accept and forgive unconditionally. Yourself first. Then others.

MY "EXITPOINT"

March 26, 2015

It was a chilly grey rainy day in Charlotte, NC. I was at home doing what flight attendants do on those days in between flying trips, when I got one of those little "cosmic nudges" that I never ignore anymore. I pay close attention to whatever I am being directed to do or go wherever I am being directed to go. It may not make any sense to me until after I have completed my "mission," but I always get the understanding behind it within a day or so. I may be directed to get on a plane and fly to Phoenix or somewhere sunny in order to just be there, get some sun, read, and be mindless. I never know the reason nor do I question it. I have no need to know "why."

Sometimes I rent a car and drive to wherever it is I am guided to go. Typically they are pretty long drives, sometimes to some nondescript town or area or historic site away from "civilization," where I have access to a hotel. Sometimes I don't rent a car and just stay at a hotel near the airport for a couple of days, having no clue as to why but knowing that it will be revealed to me at some point.

During one visit to Phoenix a few years ago, I was nudged to go to Phoenix for a couple of days. The last thing I want to do on my days off is to be in the middle of the flying public, get on a plane, and fly across the country for a couple of days. Once again, I learned many years ago not to ignore these cosmic nudges, and so I packed up my swimming trunks (in the middle of the summer I might add. Frying pan hot in Phoenix.)

On day two of "just being there," getting ready to head out to the pool with my latest murder detective story, traveling out-of-body in the sun when I wasn't reading, zipping around different dimensions and having a big old time, I walked down to a nearby convenience store to get a cold drink before my day in the sun.

As usually happens before a moment in time when I am "placed" in a situation where my gifts kick in and I am to serve someone with them, the divine arranges for the moment to be ideal for me to serve the person as best I can. In this case, I got my 44-ounce drink with a lot of crisp crunchy ice, walked up to the counter, and noticed that the other shoppers in the store had gone, leaving just the cashier and I.

As I walked up to pay I knew at that moment exactly why I had made the trip to Phoenix, and it was this brief 4 or 5 minutes speaking with the cashier. I will not go into all of the details here, but to sum it up...Her mother was actively dying. She had been in hospice care for the past several days, and the cashier absolutely had to come to work that day, leaving her mom alone.

I gently touched her arm, gave her my card and told her things that were important for her to hear. I gave her a couple of relevant "real-time" messages from her mother that this sweet girl confirmed had to do with things that had been said just that morning before she came to work. And then she began to cry with relief and gratitude, coming around the counter and giving me a big bear hug with a huge beautiful smile and a sense that everything was going to be okay. I got a free cold drink that day and the reason for my "mission."

So, here we are on March 26, 2015, and I am being nudged again to do "something." And I pay attention.

I was being directed to get in the car and drive to Uhwharrie National Forest, about a 90-minute drive from my house. Okie dokie. Having no idea why, and knowing better than to argue with the universe, I gassed up the car and took off.

The Uhwarrie National Forest is part of the 2 million acres of public lands managed by the North Carolina Wildlife Resources Commission for year-round camping, hiking, biking, off-roading, public hunting, trapping, fishing, and other recreational activities. Around 500 million years ago the Uhwarries were a coastal mountain range thought to have once peaked at some 20,000 feet before eroding to a maximum of just over 1100 feet, and now lie 150 miles inland from the coast. It is still argued that the Uhwarries are the oldest mountain range in North America. It doesn't matter. They are still VERY old, chiseled down by erosion and time, dinosaurs roaming the mountain tops a long, long time ago. Was I getting ready to have some kind of close encounter with a holographic T-Rex from another dimension?! In any case, Google the Uhwarrie National Forest, Morrow Mountain, and the old mines in the area. It is beautiful serene country with its mysterious little nubbins of mountains in the heart of North Carolina.

I was directed to drive to one of the more primitive campgrounds, drive around the circle and park at one of the campsites. It was 11:30 in the morning and the entire campground was deserted. I parked at the campsite that the car pulled into, got out and walked down a gentle slope, fresh clean air and tall green trees all around, not so thick that I couldn't see everything around me. Birds were chattering back and forth, and frogs or toads of some kind were bantering with each other in a narrow stream just below. And then it became silent. An instant deathly silence clicked on like a light switch and nature got quiet. You can't hear silence clicking on but it is the only way I can describe it. Immediate. Instant. Like nature herself had just stopped. Interesting.

My awareness became sharp, my curiosity heightened, and with years of having "normal" experiences like this, I knew without knowing that I wouldn't be harmed, and that something pretty cool was going on here. What that was, I had no earthly idea. And that's what made it such an adventure...the NOT knowing. So, without looking for anything to happen or wondering what this may be all about, I simply set my intent to receive whatever it was that was to be revealed to me and to have clarity with its meaning whenever it was appropriate. And then I just let go of all thought, blissfully right there in the moment.

I was immersed in this delicious absolute silence for just a few minutes. Nothing happened. And then I left, heading back to Mt. Holly and whatever it was I was in the middle of before I drove over here. It was on the way home that I received the ripple of the reason for my road trip...a stretched slinky suddenly let go and catching up with itself.

I-85 west wasn't terribly busy on the drive home, yet there was a situation that got my attention and which had the potential to turn into a serious car accident, which I could have been involved in. I was in the center lane, an 18-wheeler just merging into the right lane immediately beside me. In the side mirror I saw an old beat-up minivan coming up on my left in the fast lane. No big deal...Until the driver started easing over, crossing the line into my lane at a very high speed, texting of course. Paying no attention and closing fast, and with the big rig on my right hand side, I had nowhere to go. The minivan just missed my side mirror as they finally looked up and swerved back into their lane and sped off.

I said some potty words, slowed my heart down, and at that same instant received a flash of information out of nowhere. Now this may sound bizarre to most folks and that's okay. I will do the best I can to explain in a minute. People not believing it or understanding it doesn't make the experience or information I received any less real. In the moments immediately after the swerving minivan sped away, I knew without knowing that I was supposed to have died that day. And I didn't.

The portal to my exitpoint had shifted. Do I know when or where it shifted to? Nope. All I know is that I am still here. I will continue being me, doing what I do, until I come to that portal once again. Maybe next time I will go through. We just never know. Every moment offers a wonderful opportunity to be present in this very moment with gratitude, joy, and a childlike sense of wonder and trust.

DROP into the Quantum "POUP" and Just "BE"

OTHER BOOKS BY KELI ADAMS

FRIENDLY SHADOWS

Friendly Shadows is the true story about psychic flight attendant, Keli Adams, who, along with other amazing intuitive gifts is, able to communicate with departed loved ones and pets. In *Friendly Shadows* you follow Keli's frightening childhood similar to the little boy in the movie, "The Sixth Sense," into her career as a flight attendant with a major airline beginning in 1986. In 1988, Keli's life began changing in bizarre and wonderful ways that started with a visit on the beach with her mother, Marilyn. At that point, Keli's intuitive gifts began developing quickly and have grown and been fine-tuned in wondrous and healing ways over the years, up to her incredible life she lives now. Marilyn writes the last few chapters of *Friendly Shadows* in her delightful and loving voice, helping the reader understand that we live on beyond physical death. You see, Keli's mother, Marilyn, passed away in 1963 when Keli was just a young child. Together they have written a little book of hope, bridging two different worlds, showing how we can all keep the connection to those we have loved and seemingly have lost. We don't die and our loved ones are just a thought, just a breath away. Marilyn shows you how to keep that connection yourself, without the aid of a spirit communicator to intercede.

Whatever you believe – is.

Angels in the Flesh / Spirits in Spirals

Flight attendants and today's flying public are sometimes a very interesting mix. The airline industry and the world are becoming a little too crazy. In _Angels in the Flesh/Spirits in Spirals,_ two books under one cover, find a little grain of sanity through humor, heart and spirit. Flight attendant, Keli Adams, takes you on hysterical adventures through her world of the airline industry, as well as journeys to spirit and heart while walking labyrinths, ancient tools of meditation and enlightenment.

Ethan's Milagro
A Place Where Souls are Fed - Hearts Sing - and You are the Miracle

Ethan's Milagro is the true story of an amazing relationship between a psychic flight attendant, Keli Adams, and two-year-old Ethan, born with a limiting genetic condition. Ethan is unable to communicate well, but he laughs a lot. Keli communicates very well with dead people, live people and animals. She laughs a lot, too. In her first book, _Friendly Shadows,_ you learn about her frightening childhood and the development of her intuitive gifts.

She and Ethan have connected on a rare spiritual level to write this children's book for adults for everyone to deal with life, death and loss through the child-like innocence that lives within us all. Nothing can destroy it. We have just forgotten where we put it.

Ethan and Keli have created a wondrous healing park called "Milagro" where you find your innocence and your heart. Leave your "humanness" at the gate, enter with the heart of a child...play...heal... believe.

Ethan's Milagro was written in nine weeks, a full month before Ethan and Keli ever met in person. This was the only time they have ever seen each other...in person.

Black Tomatoes Purple Carrots

"The moment I scrolled down and saw the now familiar name come up on the computer screen, the hellish storm let loose its fury, reaching through the screen, wrapping its sharp claws around my disbelieving heart, and squeezing the very life out of my soul. The seething storm had found me, enshrouding me in the thick heavy bleakness of its dark icy cloak. It was dragging me impersonally through non-existent time, spiraling me down into its lair of perfect nothingness, showing no feeling or conscience. The unholy tempest now had a name, and its name was death."

Written in a unique format, colorful stories of the airline industry, the war in Iraq, online dating, quaint tiny towns in Kansas, magical Clydesdales, and desperately trying to find sanity in an insane world, weave the reader masterfully into the very soul of this amazing fabric of complex situations and interesting people. More truth than fiction, Keli Adams, flight attendant, author, intuitive healer, and paranormal investigator, has created a rich word tapestry that wraps the reader in a brilliant silky palette of swirling emotions. And then there is the ending.

Psychic Grace

Psychic Grace is a work of "faction," which is fiction based on fact. All of the characters in the book are based on people in Keli's life. She really is a flight attendant and hospice volunteer who communicates with the actively dying on powerful and amazing nonverbal levels. Through time spent with her actual patients, Keli communicates how to appreciate the simple joys of life; she dispels fears of the dying process, showing how to live in the present moment. Through these beautiful (and sometimes quite entertaining) souls she was able to spend time with, she offers the comforting perception that we indeed survive physical "death."

Atchison Kansas - Portal to Other Worlds

Atchison, Kansas, purported to be the most haunted town in Kansas, has been a fascination to Keli since 1994, In this fun little book, Keli offers some of Atchison's rich and colorful history and why the town is so "haunted." She offers possible scientific reasons as to why many places in town may be actively "spirited" but not haunted. As a paranormal researcher with over 30 years of experience, Keli gives you information in this book for you to conduct your own "ghost hunt" to discover the difference between haunted and spirited.